FACING LIFE'S PROBLEMS

No one gets a trouble-free life; so we must face reality

Timeless counsel and wisdom by

Bob Garon

First printing: 1981
Second printing: 1982
Third printing: 1986
Revised edition: 1995 and 1996

Published by VGV PUBLICATIONS

Printed in the United States of America.

Cover layout and internal formatting: Francisca de Zwager

For information: P.O Box MCPO 2099, Makati City, Sen Gil Puyat Avenue, Makati City, Philippines, 1260
or www.facebook.com/bobgaron

ISBN: 978-1-7378277-1-9

Royalties earned from this book will help poor children in the Philippines get an education.

To all those whom I love
and who have loved me

Contents

Foreword

My husband's favorite song during his evening radio counseling program many years ago was Barbara Streisand's song "People." It reflected how much he loved people. All his life, Bob aimed to touch others through his counseling and his writing in his daily columns in various newspapers and publications.

During the 44 years that I lived with him and loved him, I witnessed his gift of helping people who encountered serious life problems. He simply had an exceptional way of making a tough problem more manageable. After a brief talk with him, one could feel the comfort that all will be well, and that there was hope for things to get better.

It is with this background that I invite you to read his book. All of us, one way or the other, have to overcome many of life's problems. Often, we feel lost and discouraged. Bob's sage advice is based on actual life experiences that touched and made an imprint in Bob's heart and psyche. The articles in this book, first published in 1981, are deep, meaningful, and today still completely relevant. I hope you will find wisdom and relief from whatever challenges you have to face in life.

After all, for as long as we live, problems are part of our daily lives. His articles are short and easy to understand. He used to tell me, "When I write, I always aim to communicate directly with my readers." He desired to give his readers consolation and compassion so they could face squarely their problems with relative ease.

I end by encouraging you that *everything is possible*. Life is worthwhile if we do not run away from our problems.

Emmy Garon
(Philippines, 2022)

Preface

I have a theory about Bob's magnificent neuroses. The main theme which has always fascinated him, even before I discussed it with him, is the central theme of human drama–that of temptation, fall and redemption. In the case of DARE, he was attracted to the vision of man redeeming himself in the eyes of peers and of society and therefore in his own eyes. This fascination, I think, led him to choose the self- help type of rehabilitation program that he found in Daytop. That DARE's favorite song is "The Impossible Dream" is not an accident. The lyrics extol the struggle of man against tremendous odds--including his own infirmity. Neither was it an accident that I heard this song sung with feeling by more than a hundred ex-addicts one evening a year ago; each one knew that it was his life, his song. At that moment, I noticed the audience joining in, including myself. A glimpse perhaps of one facet of humanity that Bob perceived intuitively - the cry to rise up again and try to reach for the unreachable star is one of the most moving messages for man because it is his story. The author and all the young people in DARE have known life as it is; Bob inspires them to see and live life as it should be.

Almost completely without formal training in the behavioral sciences, Bob started a rehabilitation center for drug dependents here in the Philippines, and guided it to growth and acceptance by this society. Like all things new and innovative, the program and the Founder met with tremendous resistance- some painful and personal. He is not a masochist; I have seen him hit right back. But only in the privacy of his office. His daily column in the Daily Express continued to dwell on people, on drugs occasionally; and mostly just reflecting the inner nature of the author. It is a measure of the man that not once, even under unjust provocation, has he made use of his articles or his TV shows to strike back at his tormentors.

Many of the articles in this book came from these periods of personal difficulty for the author. Often, they are in the form of advices to himself. The how-to-solve-your-problem genre of writing has been over-published. If this book differs from the others, it does so in ways that, I suspect, many others who bought his other books like.

Firstly, Bob writes from day to day - if he has advice to give, it is probably advice that he used himself yesterday or that morning, and found effective. It is written in the spirit of sharing with his fellow mortals and not as a guru to his disciples.

Secondly, I observed that his readers perceive and react to something beyond the substance of what is written. It is not just style. It is the mystery that passes between a good therapist and his patients. Some call this the basically non-judgmental and compassionate attitude within the therapist himself and his willingness to share, with great honesty, his feelings with others.

Thirdly, he carries no suffix to his name, no M.D., no Ph.D. As all physicians and psychologists know, we learn from our patients. I suggested to Bob that he include some statistics compiled by his secretary: literally thousands of hours of counselling a wide variety of cases handled over radio, on TV, personally in his different rehabilitation centers, or in the privacy of his small office. He just smiled and waved the idea away. He was thinking about another unreachable star.

Theodore B.R Abas, M.D.
Psychiatric Consultant
DARE Foundation, Inc.

Author's Note

If you are reading this book in order to find some kind of magic formula which will ensure a trouble-free life, you will surely be disappointed. There is no way that you can avoid problems because trouble is part of the fabric of life. Wherever you go, whoever you are, whatever your station in life; you can be sure that you will run into problems regularly until your dying day.

There are many reasons why it is impossible to avoid problems. Some of them will be discussed in the following pages. But basically, the reason is that reality refuses to bow before our wills. It is inflexible and unyielding. It is harsh and uncompromising.

Problems stem from our inability to recognize reality and its many complex features. We often find it difficult to see the difference between what is real and what is the creation of our thinking. What causes problems is the clash between the real out there and our unreal way of perceiving reality. Reality refuses to conform to our way of thinking. And that is where the initial trouble begins.

There are, on the other hand, many persons who do not recognize reality for what it is and they cannot seem to cope with it, especially the hard aspects of it. They have a low stress level. Their capacity to deal with frustration is not adequate. In short, reality kicks them around, and they are virtually helpless to do anything about it.

I believe that people are unhappy because they lack the necessary tools with which to cope with unpleasant reality. They are often defenseless against brutal reality. They do not know what to do when harsh moments are upon them. They become numb and are unable to move. They stand around in a confused state of mind, not knowing which direction to take. It is in times like this that reality knocks them over because they stand in its way.

The secret of happy living lies in accepting and knowing. Accepting the fact that trials, troubles and difficulties spare no man and are as inevitable as the sunrise. Knowing how to face these hardships and disappointments without going to pieces. More than that, it means realizing that problems are usually blessings in disguise if one can effectively handle them. The wise and mature individual can most often turn them into growth-giving experiences.

If you have learned how to accept the reality of trouble in your life; if you have learned how to deal with it effectively; then you can be relatively happy.

If you can remember that no man is the master of reality because no individual can possess all the truth, then, you will not be discouraged when those inevitable feelings of depression strike. You must understand that it will take a lifetime of learning (much of it the hard way) before you can deal effectively with life's harshness. There are no quick solutions, no one way of doing things.

Each one of us must find which way is best suited to his particular personality and disposition.

We must understand that since there is no avoiding life's problems, knowledge and skills for dealing with them are not enough. We must possess a healthy dose of courage and faith. Courage to rise up and stand our ground and not succumb to the strong temptation to break and run for cover. Confidence in ourselves and our ability to live harmoniously with reality. Faith in a Power greater than us that cares and watches over our destinies.

This book is a feeble attempt to give a few insights into the many complexities of living. It does not pretend to give any answers. It is my hope and prayer that these pages will set the reader to simply thinking for himself about facing life's problems. Once this is done, the first step has been taken. If what I have written can give even a few clues about effectively dealing with the problems of life, then I shall be happy.

Bob Garon

IN SEARCH OF HAPPINESS

Every single person on this planet is in search of happiness. Happiness (whatever that may be) is something that people will do anything and everything to have. There are those who rob banks, swindle people, and do all kinds of things in order to get money because they believe that happiness is found in wealth. There are as many places to look for happiness as there are people; as many ideas about happiness as there are individuals.

Very few people thoroughly understand that happiness is not a place, a thing, or a person, but a state of mind. Happiness resides in a man's head and in his heart. It is an interior thing. Two people suffer from the same disease: one is totally unhappy and spends his day cursing his misfortune; the other radiates a kind of joy that causes wonder and amazement in all who see him. Here is an unhappy man who has everything that money can buy. There is a poor "basurero" who seems to be happy and content with the little that he has.

Why is it like this? Why is it that some people seem to find happiness quickly and easily and others can never seem to even come close to it? Why is it that some can almost create happiness upon request, whereas others have to go through great and complex processes before coming up with even a little bit of joy and satisfaction? It is because virtually all human unhappiness (or happiness) is caused and sustained by the view one takes of things rather than the things themselves.

Reality is unchanging. It is the same for everybody. When the rains come and the streets get flooded, everybody gets wet. However, there are those who curse the rains, and there are those who couldn't care less if it rains or if the sun shines; and there are those who enjoy frolicking in the rain. It all depends on the view one takes of the rain, rather than the rain itself.

And it is like this all through life. A man loses his wife. He is now a widower with five children. He can either turn to the bottle and drown himself in self-pity or he can seriously get down to the task of taking care of his five kids. The individual with terminal cancer can either curse God or graciously accept the reality of death. The wealthy man who loses his fortune can either blow his brains out or get busy rebuilding his business.

THE ABCs OF HAPPINESS

EVERYBODY WANTS to be loved. That is a normal, natural and valid desire. I have often written about this need to be loved. And I believe that all I have said still holds true.

However, there are some people who feel that it is an absolute necessity to be loved and to gain approval of everyone for everything they do. Now, this is a different story. Children and teenagers have this unrealistic desire to be loved by the whole world. They hope to get the approval of just about anybody who means anything to them. As they grow and mature, they soon discover that this is impossible; one cannot be loved by everybody. Neither can a man who is doing something worthwhile gain the approval of all his peers.

Human beings are complex creatures. Their minds work in strange ways. None of them is totally predictable in his behavior. It is inevitable that conflicts of interest will arise between people in their day-to-day relationships. One can be just as sure that divergent thoughts and opinions will give rise to hard feelings and hurt sensitivities. Just as one cannot possibly find the time nor the energy to love everybody, in the same vein, one cannot expect to be loved and cared for by everyone he meets. Besides, I doubt if anybody could respond to so much loving.

As a person matures, he understands this and is resigned to the fact that he is not loved by most people. He may have many casual friends and acquaintances but the real loving will be limited to those who mean something to him. He knows that perhaps a few people will hate him, and a number will love him, while most will remain quite indifferent to him. This is the way things have always been, are now, and perhaps will always be. The sooner an individual learns to accept the reality, the sooner he becomes liberated from the tyranny of trying to please everybody.

But there are those who insist on being loved by all. They get tremendously upset when somebody who really means nothing to them shows dislike or disgust for them. They sink into deep depression when people who are relatively unknown to them and whom they do not love at all disagree with them and disapprove of their behavior. This is, of course, a childish reaction, something that they have never outgrown. It is also indicative of great insecurity and immaturity. These people are also very unhappy since their efforts to gain the approval of everybody never succeeds. They seem to be constantly running around in circles and getting nowhere with people. Their friendships usually lack depth and remain on a superficial level. They over-indulge in self-pity and self-depreciation. Since they are too sensitive to the criticism of people who do not matter, they can never seem to gain a healthy amount of self-esteem. They spend too much time focusing on what is wrong with themselves and neglect to look at what they have going in their favor. This leads to a reinforcement of their low self-concept.

Mature thinking calls for an understanding of the fact that no matter who you are or what you say; no matter what you do or how much you love, there will be those who understand and love you, and those who will dislike you and refuse to love you. The vast majority of people will be indifferent and will not really care what happens to you one way or the other. If a man learns to live with this reality, then he will gain a whole lot of peace of mind. He will go about concentrating on improving his relationships and deepening his friendships with those who matter to him. He will learn how not to get upset over the hostility and indifference of the others.

More than anything else, he will remember that no matter what you do, you can never please everybody. He will become totally convinced of this truth. It will help him do what he thinks is right and to never mind what "they will say". He will concentrate on his own self-respect, on winning approval, sometimes from the people who matter and on loving rather than being loved.

HAPPINESS IS A STATE OF MIND

MAN WILL DO ANYTHING to get it. It is the primary purpose of living. Without it, he is reduced to mere existence. Everything he does, his every action is aimed at acquiring it. If he goes without it for any length of time, he thinks of blowing his brains out.

What is it? *Happiness.*

We live in a world of five billion humans, each one searching in his own way for that elusive happiness he believes will make his life worthwhile. Yet, it is amazing how few people can truthfully say that they are truly happy.

Perhaps it is because men do not really understand what happiness is all about. There are those who believe happiness is a thing. The more things one acquires, the happier one will be. Well, that is what they expect to happen. These people usually wait forever to be happy because happiness does not come with the acquisition of anything. The countless unhappy rich around us can attest to that. They are still searching and have realized that happiness is not a thing.

Then, there are those who think that happiness is a place. They believe that if they can get to the States, they will find happiness. Or perhaps if they could someday move into Forbes Park, they would find happiness there. Wrong again.

Others believe that happiness is a person. If only he could marry that attractive beauty queen, the young man believes that his happiness will be complete. If only the wife could get her husband back, she would be happy again. That's what she thinks! Happiness is not a thing, a place, or a person. What is it then? I say it is a ***state of mind***.

There are people who are as poor as church mice and who are very happy. I know people who live in distant barrios and who are happy. And there are men who are happily married to women who are as ugly as the seven capital sins.

What all have in common is contentment. This is the secret of happy living. To be content. If one can be content with one's situation in life, one can find happiness.

Easier said than done. We never seem to be contented. We spend our days dreaming about what could be instead of enjoying what is. There is an undeniable suffering in longing.

We cannot seem to enjoy what we have and with whom we are with. We keep having second thoughts about everything and everyone.

If only we could learn to enjoy the NOW in life. I'm not saying we should not plan ahead and look to the future in order to better our lot. Of course, we should. But we shouldn't get sick over it. Planning should not prevent us from enjoying our day today. After all, yesterdays are dead and gone. Tomorrows exist only in the mind of God. It would be a tragedy if we were so focused on the past and the future that we would forget living today. It would be terrible if we could never find at least some degree of contentment in the many blessings we have already received.

In final analysis, your happiness (or lack of it) will depend wholly on you. If you want to be happy, nobody can prevent you from being so. If you insist on being miserable, even God won't change that. It's all up to you. There are dying men in cancer wards who end their days with a smile on their lips and there are those who leave this world whispering curses.

If you insist on making yourself happy, you can learn to smile and find joy even in the midst of great suffering. If you want misery to be your constant companion, you won't even manage a smile on your honeymoon. The choice is yours to make: happiness or depression. Choose.

HAPPINESS IS...

I HAVE OFTEN SAID that the reason people are so unhappy is that they never seem to be satisfied with what they are and what they have. They spend far too much time-wasting precious moments and energy thinking about what might have been. They indulge in useless and even destructive daydreaming. Happy people, whether rich or poor, are those who can gain satisfaction in what they are and in what they are doing. The shoeshine boy may be a whole lot happier than the "successful" businessman who lives in the lofty mansion. The farmer who is constantly struggling with the land in order to eat might not want to change places with the supervisor of a big office.

It is not what you do that makes you happy or unhappy. What gives joy or sadness is the attitude that you carry through life. There are rich men who are miserable because they can never seem to come to grips with themselves and find peace of heart in what they are doing. On the other hand, there are much less "fortunate" persons who seem to exude a joy that is difficult for more troubled people to understand.

Bob Garon

I suppose you could say that it is all in the mind. It depends on how you look at life and your relation to it.

Happiness is not a place or a circumstance. It is rather a state of mind. You can create your own happiness or you can refuse to have anything to do with it. It's really up to you.

Perhaps the most important thing to do is to look at yourself realistically. See your potentials and limitations. Then, try to live with them. There can be only one president of the country. In the army, there must be few generals and lots of sergeants and privates. Not everyone can be a hotel manager. Somebody has got to wash the dishes.

Not all men are called to lead or to specialize or to become professionals. The genius who will rise to great heights in the arts and sciences is rare. Many are called to be laborers in factories, fields, and streets. But all work is significant because it is undertaken by that noble creature - Man. The great Martin Luther King, Jr. said it well: "All labor that uplifts humanity has dignity and importance and should be undertaken with painstaking excellence. If a man is called to be a street sweeper, he should sweep the streets even as Michelangelo painted or Beethoven composed music or Shakespeare wrote poetry. He should sweep streets so well that all the hosts of heaven and earth will pause to say, 'Here lived a great street sweeper who did his job well.'"

What is most important is to enjoy doing whatever you set out to do. See meaning in whatever you do, and then do it with enthusiasm.

The poet Douglas Mallock put it beautifully when he wrote:

"If you can't be a pine on top of the hill
Be a scrub in the valley - but be
The best little scrub by side of the hill.
Be a bush, if you can't be a tree.
If you can't be a highway, just be a trail;
If you can't be the sun; be a star;
It isn't by size that you win or fail.
Be the best of whatever you are."

UNHAPPINESS STEMS FROM PEOPLE

THE KEY TO HAPPY living is people and one's ability to live with them successfully. Rich or poor, privileged or unfortunate, when a man has many friends, he surely possesses a kind of wealth that cannot be bought.

People are unhappy because they fail in their relationships with others or they are not as successful in love and friendship as they would like to be. Any way you look at it, a man's unhappiness always stems from something that went wrong with his dealings with people.

Married people have problems that almost always have something to do with their partners. Problems of how to increase an already deep love, various threats to their love relationship, etc.

The more capable a person is in understanding others and applying that knowledge, the greater are his chances of being happy. A woman may not be good looking at all and yet be loved deeply and consequently enjoy great happiness. I guessed it all depends on how she accepts the reality that she is not physically attractive. If she can see beyond the "Mascara" and realize there is a lot more to being loved than the way one's face is formed, then she stands a good chance of being happy. If, on the other hand, she allows her homeliness to make her bitter against the world, then you cannot expect people to be drawn to someone who is always crying over things that cannot be changed.

There is much to learn about people. And since they are the key to our happiness, we should be more than eager to understand them. The first thing we must learn is to become very sensitive to the needs of others.

A DARE resident slipped a beautiful prayer under my door the other night. It was written by Norman Vincent Peale and I want to share it with you.

"O Lord, grant that each one who has to do with me today may be happier for it. Let it be given to me each hour today what I shall say, and grant me the wisdom of a loving heart and that I may say the right thing rightly.

Help me to enter into the mind of everyone who talks with me, keep me alive to the feelings of each one present. Give me a quick eye for the little kindnesses that I may be ready in doing them and gracious in receiving them.

Give me a quick perception of the feelings and needs of others, and make me eager-hearted in helping them. Amen."

MAN MUST HAVE A PURPOSE

WHEN A MAN CAN find no meaning to his life, he is in deep trouble. He may not know it. He might even deny it. However, this lack of awareness does not lessen his problem. On the contrary, it renders him even more vulnerable.

One common denominator that can be found in every drug abuser when he comes to DARE is the lack of meaning in his life. In fact, we spend countless hours helping young people in their search for meaning. As long as a youngster continues to float in life, he remains in trouble. He either becomes listless or throws himself headlong into all kinds of empty activities. His interest in school falls. Why should he study when he fails to see the point of it all? He cannot keep a job for very long. Why should he work when he sees no purpose to his sweat and sacrifices?

A surprising number of drug abusers have made attempts at suicide. I am not astonished at this fact because suicide makes a lot of sense to people who can find little or no meaning to life. In fact, when a man is suffering and cannot understand the why of it all, suicide is a convenient way out of a painful and a confusing situation.

I don't think that you will ever find the man with a purpose in life wanting to blow his brains out. That just does not happen. The individual who has found a meaning of life wants to live his life to the fullest. He enjoys it. He does not want it to end because he finds so much sense to what he is doing.

I have seen how young people have been transformed overnight when they suddenly found a meaning to their existence. Apathy and listlessness vanish. They immediately stop wandering aimlessly. They move faster. There is a newfound sense of purpose that permeates all their actions. They seem to live again. Suicide is the farthest thing from their minds.

I fully subscribe to Dr. Victor Frankl's theory that the key to a happy life lies in man's finding a purpose. Perhaps it's because this has been my experience. There have been moments in my life when I have felt that living hardly made any sense at all. In times such as these, I lost all enthusiasm. Life became a drag. Doing the simplest thing was difficult. I became conscious of how long were my days.

All that changed when I suddenly discovered newfound meaning in what I was doing. Then brightness shone through. Smiles became easy and my footsteps were light. The changes were due to a new sense of purpose.

Bob Garon

People are unhappy because they fail to see the purpose and the meaning in what they are doing and because of this, they are not really and truly living but merely existing. It is only when men become aware of the need to have a purpose in life that they feel restless enough to search for it. Otherwise, they simply float through the many years of their lives without direction, without purpose, and without meaning. Man's search for meaning goes on and it is only man himself, says Dr. Frankl, who can find his own direction. Others may help him, guide him and encourage him; however, in the end, man must discover for himself the true meaning of his existence. Only then will he achieve that degree of happiness that he so desperately aspires to possess. Only then will life make any sense to him at all.

WHAT LIFE IS ALL ABOUT

IF YOU CAN NEVER seem to gain satisfaction from life, chances are you are full of regrets. If you keep looking over the fence, contemplating the greenness in the other fellow's yard, you are undoubtedly a very unhappy man. If you keep feeling sorry for yourself and thinking about what might have been, I'm sure that happiness is, for you, a very elusive thing.

Life is unpredictable. It is also complex. There are some things in life that we can control. There are happenings that, in spite of all our efforts, cannot be avoided. Every man is, to a certain extent, the master of his own destiny. There are things that he can make happen. He can set goals for himself. He has free will which allows him to decide many things for himself. In this sense, he is own master.

However, there are moments when his decisions do not bear fruit. There are times when a man makes the wrong move and ends up regretting his decision. Often, his mistake is his failure to decide anything at all. He simply stands around, trying to make up his mind. In the end, his inaction causes him to spend much of his time daydreaming.

I believe that a tremendous amount of unhappiness is caused by what I call the inability to get on with the business of life. What I mean by this is that some people are so taken up with regrets about the past that they cannot seem to function in the present. They weep over the misfortunes of yesterday. When they think of the chances that they missed, they kick the wall in disgust. They constantly use expressions like "I could have," "I should have," "If only I had". Ask them if they could live their lives over again, would they change anything, and you are sure to get the reply "I would change everything."

People like this go through happy life with a frown and inevitably die very unhappy. Perhaps it is because they never can get in touch with what living is all about. In a way, I guess you could say that they are living on the edge of reality. If they only understood that life is short, too short to waste it on regrets and wishful thinking, then perhaps they would begin to see the beauty of their lives.

I can't remember who said it, but I jotted down the words of a man who understood what living is all about. I would like to share them with you.

"Not by what might have been or could have been will the glory of this battle be judged.

The wind could very well have blown this way.

The rain might very well have come today.

No room for regrets,

No time for misgivings

But for doing what should be done here and now, hour by hour.

One day we might say:
We did not waste our time in unless dreaming.
We fought out battles day to day,
Accepting losses as well as winnings.
We are what we are,
Not for what might have been,
Or could have been,
But for what we made it be."

LIFE IS FULL OF UPS AND DOWNS

People I meet often ask the old familiar question we have all heard a thousand times.

"How's life?"

Most answer: "Fine." I usually say: "Full of ups and downs - but mostly downs." They smile. Little do they suspect that I'm not joking.

It is not that I am a pessimist, because I am not. I certainly would never have stuck my neck out and gotten involved so often if I was. I rather like to think of myself as a realist.

I have lived 57 years, and I must say that they have been, for the most part, uneventful years. I think I had a pretty ordinary life as a farm boy and a student back in the States.

I have had my little thrills (I won my share of baseball, basketball, and football games) and I have known the feeling of the defeated and the discouraged (I spent two years in grade four and graduated from elementary school number 84 in a class of 85). So, I am no different from any of you. There are moments in my life when the sun shines brightly and there are times when dark clouds hang overhead.

Today, at this writing, my sky is overcast and the air is heavy with discouragement. Why? Well, I guess I could say that it is just one of those things. One of the projects in which I am involved suffered a setback. People just do not seem to understand what I am trying to say. And it looks like I have wasted a lot of time and breath and energy trying to get through to people I felt understood my message. It was made clear to me today that they did not understand at all.

"Life is full of ups and downs - mostly downs" is what I always say. Of course, I believe that is not true. I know there are moments of joy and times of sadness in every man's life. But what I do NOT believe is that sad events take up "most" of our time. In fact, I think that we are relatively happy most of the time.

However, we usually tend to magnify our "downs" and take for granted the "ups" we encounter. Perhaps it is because we expect to be happy all the time. We have such a low threshold of pain that we feel we have to complain. Or maybe we always draw more attention to our disappointments.

What I'm trying to say is this: no matter who we may be or where we are, there will always be some dark moments. The sooner we resign ourselves to this undeniable fact, the sooner we will find that peace of mind that everybody talks about, but few people ever possess.

I have just begun to understand this myself. I now realize that life is like the weather. There is the dark night and the bright day. The darkness helps me to better understand the light. There is sunshine and there is rain. Too much sunshine causes a man to dry up, wither and die. Rain is needed to make a man grow in wisdom and in stature. There is the calm and there is the storm. The calm permits a man to build while the storm puts to the test what he has constructed.

Whenever I feel the way I am feeling right now, I say to myself: "Hold on tightly for a few hours more, Bob. Just wait a while and it will be morning and the sun will shine again."

When I feel myself buffeted by strong winds, I do what the mariner does… I ride out the storm and hang on hopefully, because I know that typhoons do not last forever.

LIFE IS A BIG GAMBLE

BRUCE LEE ONCE made a statement which I believe holds true in my own life. "It's not important how long you live," he said, "It's what you accomplish during your life that matters." I have often said I would rather live a short and exciting life than experience 80 years of boredom.

I see life as being so short that the most precious of possessions is time. Without time, you can do nothing. Sufficient time is what allows a man to do what he's always wanted to do.

Life for me is a big gamble. Either I will be very happy and deeply satisfied or I will live miserably with a million regrets. Happiness depends on one's ability to make decisions-the right ones. So many people are unhappy because they keep thinking of what might have been had they not missed the golden opportunities that presented themselves.

To live a life of regrets is to guarantee restlessness and discontent. The key to happiness lies in having the courage to weigh matters and then to decide correctly.

Happiness in this life belongs to the skillful decision-makers. Every day, we are faced with situations that call for decisions. Mature people are those who can make up their minds, and not be sorry later.

This, however, is not always easy. Deciding something will naturally bring about some kind of consequences. And things do not often work out the way we would like them to. Yet, this is where the mature man shows his mettle. He is quick to adapt to the newly created crisis. He makes other decisions that hopefully see him through the thick of things.

The ability to decide is what gets people involved. There are many individuals who cannot really make decisions and who, in the end, never decide one way or the other. They are the ones who forever find themselves on the sidelines watching all the action take place before them, but never getting into battle. I think that they feel miserable about themselves because I believe they really want to get involved. However, because of fear, they do not dare make a move.

Also, there comes a time in every man's life when he feels he MUST make a decision and get involved regardless of the circumstances, or sacrifice his dignity as a human being. When this moment is upon him, he must decide to make a move or he will have to learn to live with himself, knowing that he lacked the courage to act.

Some people get into the habit of "playing it safe" and never risk involvement unless they absolutely have to. Others, like Bruce Lee, give it all they've got and plunge headlong into life. These would surely agree with this master of the martial arts when he said that it's not how long you live, but what you do with your life that counts.

LIFE MUST HAVE DIRECTION

THE OTHER DAY, as I was sitting at a friend's desk. I saw a paper under the glass which said: "TODAY is TODAY. Today is here. I will start it with a smile and resolve to be agreeable. I will not criticize. I will refuse to waste my valuable time. Today has one thing in which I know I am equal with others - ***time***. All of us draw the same salary in seconds, minutes, hours. Today, I will not waste my time because the minutes I wasted yesterday are as lost as a vanished thought."

This passage got me to thinking about life and the way we look at it and live it. Most people who sleep eight hours a day spend one third of their lives in bed asleep. We all use up about three hours a day eating. Another hour at least is given over personal needs. All this means that just about half of the day is usually spent eating and sleeping. If a man lives to be 50, he has spent 25 years asleep and sitting at the dinner table.

The way I see it, that doesn't leave much time to live - unless your idea of living means eating and sleeping. God ordained things this way though, and who are we to question His wisdom. Maybe He gave us half of our lives to rest and nourish our bodies because it is His wish that we be strong enough to do something constructive with the other half. Yet, it is amazing how people see their lives in different lights. For some, living is embodied in the pursuit of pleasure in all its forms. They have no direction and no goals. For others, there is no choice but to spend life wholly trying to survive and help those loved ones to eat. Theirs is usually an unhappy life. Then, there are those who live their lives for others; some in a dramatic way, others in a quiet and silent manner.

I suppose it all depends on how you look at life. For those who are dedicated to the service of others, there can be no other way to live, although many may call them foolish. Perhaps the formula for right living is written in the sky. Maybe the answer cannot be found in this life. Perhaps we will know how we should have lived only when there is no more living to do.

GOD MADE US THE WAY WE ARE

IT'S 10 P.M. at the moment, as I sit in my study and begin these lines, I'm very irritated and angry. At who? At myself. Why? Because I talk too much. Just a while ago, I bumped into a couple in my sala. I didn't really want to talk to them because I had a deadline to meet and I felt it might take time.

I told myself I would get down to the heart of the matter quickly, and then get things over with in short order before locking myself up in my study. Well, it took an hour and a half to get things "over with". What makes me mad at myself is that I could have cut the conversation short and kept it down to twenty minutes. But I didn't.

And that's why I'm sore at myself. I've always had a big mouth and I still do. For years I tried to deny it. I have finally admitted it. But I haven't yet accepted it. I believe that's why I'm upset.

I remember when I was a teenager how I used to hate myself for having spoken out of line so often and so disastrously. I used to hate my big mouth and vowed countless times to become a man of silence. It never happened. I haven't stopped talking since. All too often, I still say the wrong things at the right time.

I'm not making any excuses, but I believe that I shall be a big mouth all my life until I die of throat cancer because God created me thus. Just as I admire men of few words (meaningful words, that is) there are those people who marvel at the endless thoughts that pour forth from my mouth with relative ease. The quiet and shy types wish they could talk and they suffer because of their inability to communicate properly. Those who talk too much suffer because their own words are used against them.

All my life, I've wanted to be a "cool person" whose patience is inexhaustible. The fact is that I'm very emotional (often hotheaded) and patience is the least of my virtues.

I remember getting thrown out of six basketball games during my senior year in high school. The reason: fighting. After those games, I hated myself so much that I would vow never to play again. As much as I admired them, I could not understand how my teammates could lose so calmly. It was aggressiveness. I never did master my temper, although I have been able to tone it down considerably. I always wanted to do well in mathematics. I tried. God knows how hard I tried. Results: I flunked my math consistently and today I will use my fingers to count.

What I have slowly come to realize is that God made me the way I am for reasons I shall never know in this life. He destined me to be a big mouth, hotheaded, impatient, aggressive, dumb mathematician. I thank Him for putting some good qualities into the mix that became Bob.

Someday, when I have fully accepted myself after changing what I could change, I may achieve that peace of heart I desire so deeply. Till then I'll try to live with myself. It won't be easy, but then, think of those who live with me.

WE ALL HAVE A BIT OF GOD IN US

WHILE VISITING with my brother in Montreal, Canada, I was introduced to a friend of his. She was a pretty young lady of foreign descent who had come to Canada six years before.

I won't forget this young woman for a long time because she has just about the worst possible self-image. She looks at herself in a horrible way. She thinks of herself as the lowliest creature on the face of this planet.

And it's not humility either. It's just a refusal to see reality. She's good looking. Everybody says so. Yet, she denies it and feels that people tell her that just to please her. She's very intelligent. A scholar, she teaches at the most prestigious university in Canada. Yet, she insists that she's "not very intelligent."

Aside from an obvious fear of people, she has a pleasant personality and many sterling qualities. Yet, she denies it all and insists that she is practically nothing and a most undeserving creature indeed.

The woman had been somehow so programmed. And there is surely a long and complicated story of how she got her present state of "self-hatred." There are always countless factors that contribute to our making or unmaking.

But what is of vital importance is that we somehow form a decent image of ourselves. Most people are plagued by guilt feelings. Because of this, many individuals who are well thought of by their peers do not think highly of themselves at all.

Because of their secret guilts they believe people would easily change their minds about them if the whole truth were known. They live in fear of being discovered and ultimately rejected. They spend lots of time throwing up smoke screens in a desperate (and often futile attempt) to disguise their real selves.

The result is sometimes tragic. We are faced with wonderful people whose self-confidence is practically non-existent and who are so fearful of life that most of their potential goes unrealized. They somehow understand this yet feel helpless to do anything about it. This, in turn, only serves to reinforce the negativeness within and further convince them that they are truly (in their own words) "hopeless."

What we must all be deeply convinced of is the fact that we are made in the image and likeness of god who is love and goodness. In other words, we all have a "little bit of God in us" which makes us beautiful.

There is no man alive who is without something working in his favor. You can find goodness - and lots of it - in even the most "hopeless case".

You are your own best friend. You must love yourself. If you don't, nobody else will. People love people who care and respect themselves because they make solid friends. The one who thinks little of himself is a poor of you're looking for a minute relationship.

If you don't love yourself, don't you think it's time you started?

VIEWING EVENTS OF LIFE

THE WAY WE LOOK at the events that occur in our lives will often determine our happiness. Life is a mixture of happy events and unfortunate ones. It has its exciting moments and its dull days. Sometimes, things happen as expected. Most often, though, it is the unexpected that upsets us.

There are those among us who hope that life will be a perpetual "high". They expect a life of comparative ease that is relatively trouble-free. And when a big problem surfaces, they get confused, and do not really know what to make of it all. They are hurt, deeply hurt. They even begin to think thoughts like, "God hates me and is punishing me." They see themselves as the unluckiest people in the world. If you listen to them, you would think that they are God's neglected children.

There are others who, on the other hand, seem to be able to cope with all the hardships that make up their daily routine of living. They have the ability to bounce back after a tragedy befalls them. Although they get hurt because of the suffering that is part of their everyday life, they bear their pain with a kind of nobility and dignity that is the envy of others. When they are visited by the unexpected, they seem better able to tackle it and even flash a smile.

What is it that causes some to take life so serenely while others seem to break up under the strain of everyday living? I suppose it is a combination of a lot of things. But there is one factor that is indispensable if one is to maintain his balance in life. Unless a man understands and is firmly convinced that his life will be made up of a kaleidoscope of many kinds of happenings (some good, some unpleasant), he will surely remain confused throughout his years. Unless he expects the unexpected; unless he realizes that happy days are not forever; unless he is aware that the fabric of life is held together by pain and suffering; unless he deeply understands all these things, he will lead a miserable life and never know why.

WHAT MAKES A MAN HAPPY

I HAVE BEEN WRITING about the healthy, well-adjusted, and integrated personalities among us and have been basing my comments on the observations of Dr. Abraham Maslow, a distinguished psychologist, who has spent many years studying superior men and women and trying to understand what they are all about.

I find this extremely interesting because it gives us a chance to see what's right with people for a change. We have been spending too much time studying what's wrong with individuals. I think it's about time that we looked at those people who are well put together in order to find out what makes them tick. In this way, we can perhaps attempt to pattern our own lives after theirs in the hope of achieving that inner peace and strength of character that seems to characterize all of them.

The mature individual has a healthy respect for himself. He feels good about himself because he knows that he is adequate and competent. This in turn affords him in a deep feeling of security about himself. Such a person is known for independent thought and behavior. Although he has a deep-seated respect for others, he is not overly dependent on people. He can do without approval and recognition more than the average person. He does not desire, nor does he value superficial fame and empty honors. He perceives his own valued worth. This is enough for him.

He is in control of himself and of his destiny. He is not overwhelmed by untoward events that come into his life unexpectedly. Rather, he seems to thrive on them and makes them work to his advantage. His mistakes and failures do not discourage him. If anything, they serve to stimulate him to greater efforts. Perhaps, this is because he possesses more than enough self-confidence and faith in himself to carry him through great frustrations and disappointments.

He is not ashamed of himself. He does not make excuses for being what he is. He does not feel inferior to others, although he fully realizes that they have qualities that he does not possess. He does not feel inferior to them because he understands that he has been blessed by them because he understands that he has been blessed with characteristics that others do not have. He knows that in the end it all balances out in such a way that he remains a unique individual of great value. He realizes that he is not perfect but does not panic because of the faults and deficiencies that he sees within himself. He is well aware that this is in the nature of man and he is patiently striving to correct whatever needs to be corrected.

The psychologically healthy individual, although highly independent, enjoys the company of people. At the same time, he desires privacy. It isn't that he is running away from people or is afraid to encounter them. It is just that he desires to be alone with himself in order to more fully actualize his potentialities. These superior individuals are governed more by their own dictates rather than by what people might say."

"Since they depend less on other people." says Maslow, "they are less anxious and less hostile, less in need of their praise and their affection. They are less anxious for honors, prestige and rewards."

Dr. Maslow says that superior people are well-adjusted individuals and have what he calls "psychological freedom." They are capable of deciding for themselves even if this means making decisions that are unpopular and contrary to the opinions of most. They are not ashamed nor fearful of resisting the pressures to conform when this involves an important principle which they hold scared. They are not pretty in their ways and in their thinking. They will not argue and make a big issue out of little things such as clothes, languages, food, etc. On the other hand, they can become extremely unconventional and aggressive and contradictory when they feel basic principles are involved. They are capable of standing up to the crowd when necessary because they possess inner strength and courage, which allow them to do so.

Looking at the traits and characteristics of well-integrated, psychologically healthy individuals, I dare say that our society could use a whole lot more of these people than exist today. Let us pray that God may grant us a small army of them. Without a doubt, they could change the world and make it a much better place in which to live.

WE ALL HAVE OUR STORMS

THE KEY TO HAPPY successful living lies in the ability to bounce back. We must all be subjected to trials and tribulations in this life. It is an immutable law of living. It is a condition for our existence.

Examine the life of any human being and you will find that problems, disappointments and frustrations are part of it just as the seasons form part of the weather cycle. We all experience a dry season. There are moments in my life (and yours, too) when nothing seems to go well. There are times I feel as though I'm crossing a vast and endless desert. There is little water to refresh me. The hot sun burns up everything. There is little water to refresh me. The hot sun burns up everything. There is hardly a green leaf to be found. This is a sad moment indeed. There are days when I almost wish that I was never born. Those are trying times.

But there is also the wet season. Then the rains and the winds come. Amazing things happen. Plants and flowers spring up from what was thought to be barren and unyielding land. Everything comes alive again. There is hope and vigor everywhere.

But the rains don't come without the winds. And the winds are often destructive. High winds and strong rains have been known to wipe out whole communities.

In life, we all have our share of storms. Every so often there come into our lives strong winds that threaten to break us. Great tragedies, bitter disappointments and nagging frustration all seem to conspire to destroy our happiness.

A famous American football coach once told his team a story which I think aptly illustrates my point. "After every big storm, plenty of broken oak limbs can be found on the ground. But you never find any branches from the fir tree. Oak trees are big and strong, but they stand stiff and straight. When the wind blows, they crack. But fir trees sway with the storm and snap back afterward. Just remember: If you want to be king of the forest, you can't be too proud to bend with the wind."

There are those people who are like the oak tree. They stand stiff and proud and refuse to bend in any situation. And they do stand, at least in the light breeze. However, when the high winds come, the oak tree stands the way it has always done. It holds firm and if the wind is strong enough, the tree cracks and breaks. Then there are those who are like a fir tree. With them, flexibility is a way of life. They know how to give and take. They are humble enough to bend and bow when necessary.

More than anything else, they possess the uncanny ability to bounce back. No matter how strong the wind, however great the tragedy, they always seem to come back with a smile. Nothing seems capable of breaking them. They bounce back like a rubber ball, and the harder you seem to hit them, the higher they bounce.

Considering that we all bear some kind of suffering in life, one can see how those people are in a favorable position indeed. They somehow always find just a little bit of happiness even in the greatest tragedy. They know how to draw at least a minimum of good from the most terrible situations regardless of their hurt, their frustration, their disappointments. They seem always to be able to discern even the faintest rainbow on the horizon.

If we must suffer, then so be it. If we must be disappointed and frustrated, then I suppose there is no way to avoid it. However, we can bounce back quickly and completely. This is the secret of successful living. Blessed are those who bounce back, for they shall smile in the midst of tra

WORRY WARTS

IT IS AMAZING HOW we worry and exaggerate our fears about the future. I remember when I was still a seminarian with seven years of studies left before I could attain my goal of becoming a priest. The cold war was at its peak. I used to tell friends that I believed that I would never be ordained to priesthood because nuclear war would have wiped us all out by that time.

Well, the expected nuclear war never happened, and I was finally ordained. That was almost thirty years earlier.

I've since learned that many people have a strong tendency to exaggerate their fears about what might happen. They see the future in the darkest way. And, in spite of the fact that experience has shown them that things never (or hardly ever) end up as terrible as they expected, they find it very difficult to be optimistic about what is to come.

I remember a friend once telling me that 80 percent of the things we worry about never happen; 15 percent of the unfortunate incidents we worry about and that do take place are not nearly as expected; and we always somehow seem to survive the remaining 5 percent. My experience has proven this to be true. So many of us are "worry warts." We see trouble behind every tree in the forest. We are so lacking in self-confidence that we no longer believe in our God-given ability to successfully make our way through life.

We humans are flexible. We adapt quickly to new situations. The woman who has lost her husband is inconsolable. She sees herself as an unhappy widow who is hopelessly lost in this big world of ours without the support of the man she loved so dearly. When we look at her world crashing in on her, we wonder how she will ever survive. Somehow, though, she does get through her crisis. More than just "getting through," she finds happiness and learns to smile and to love once again.

God gave us the amazing ability to bounce back from terrible experiences. Personally, I'm in awe when I read accounts of the unbelievable suffering men and women underwent during the war. The fierce battles, the shameful concentration camps, the hunger and the humiliation; all these painful happenings caused so much grief that I wonder how the survivors can still smile. Those days must have seemed like the end of the world for some. Yet, they survived and lived to find happiness once again in spite of their scars.

Perhaps one of the most powerful indications of man's ability to meet the challenges of life with unbending optimism are the words written on the wall of Nazi death camp:

"I believe in the sun,
even when it is not shining:
I believe in love,
even if I do not feel it;
I believe in God,
even if He is silent."

WE HAVE OUR OWN TYPHOONS

THERE IS A STORM raging outside. The high winds are blowing hard. The rains are heavy. Visibility is zero. The first typhoon of the year is here and is screaming with all its might.

It has been a difficult experience, really. Last night I just about made it home. The streets were so flooded that I would have given anything to be riding in an amphibian. When I did finally get home, I was soaked to the skin. Aside from that, all my plans were disrupted. I never got to do the things that I wanted to do because the storm fouled up the lives of other people as well as my own.

Aside from the major difficulties brought about by the typhoon, there were countless minor irritants. The lights went out. The roads became impassable. Some TV stations went off the air. In short, typhoons make one's life very uncomfortable, if not miserable.

All of us have our share of typhoons in our own personal lives. We are all beset by emotional storms that cause great unhappiness. Perhaps it is the death of a loved one. Maybe it is the betrayal of a sweetheart. Or a bitter disappointment in one's work. Or perhaps it could be repeated frustrations and the inability to get an important thing done.

Whatever may be the cause, it all comes under the general heading of Hurt, Frustration, and Conflict. And no matter how long it has been since the last storm has come crashing into our lives, you can be sure that another is on the way. Storms are inevitable in day-to-day living. They come to us in regular cycles. They form an integral part of our lives, just as storms are part of the weather cycle.

There are people who do their very best to escape the emotional storms that beset us. Although they are made to experience them regularly, they refuse to truly accept the reality of them in their lives. They keep wishing and hoping against hope that their problems, difficulties, and frustrations would go away and not come back anymore. This, of course, does not happen, and they are terribly disappointed.

Then there are those who have accepted the reality of emotional storms in their lives. It's not that they enjoy them or even look forward to them. It's just that they have understood that such is a reality in their lives and no amount of wishing can change it. They expect storms to strike and to hit hard. Instead of wasting time and energy wishing that they would go away, they prepare for them. They secure themselves and take cover. And because they eventually become experts at dealing with storms, they hardly ever get caught out in the open when they do strike. In other words, they become very adept indeed at coping with problems and difficulties. Hard times do not crush them because they have become very skilled at dealing with stormy days.

I believe that this is one of the keys to happy and successful living. The man who is realistic enough to see that problems and difficulties form part of the fabric of real living will not experience as many bitter frustrations as the dreamer who tries to close his eyes in the midst of the inevitable disappointments of life. Because he is skillful at handling pain, he will get hurt less often and less seriously than he who is inexperienced in dealing with such situations.

In other words, if the winds must blow (and they must); if the floods must materialize (and they will); if things must go wrong (and there are times when they surely will); if we must experience pain (and hurt is often inevitable); then, let us stand ready. It is only in being prepared that we can minimize the devastation and the pain.

THE FLIGHT FROM REALITY

DR. BERYL D. ORRIS once wrote: "Most people are fleeing from reality because they haven't the courage to face it... If I have made the decision to live rather than to exist, then I recognize that there must be a meaning for me to have the courage to decide to live. Without meaning, there is an air of unreality about existence, and that is what makes people look for security in illusion. You see, the flight from reality becomes important to the degree that I cannot face and accept it."

Have you ever talked to someone who wanted to commit suicide? Have you ever asked a young man why he tried to kill himself? I have. And the answers are almost always the same.

I remember an accident that happened when I was a missionary in the province of Isabela. One day, I was called to the local clinic because of an emergency. When I arrived, I was met with an absolutely horrible scene. Lying on a bed before me was a naked man. I could not tell if he was young or old because he had been burned to a crisp. Every single inch of his body, from the top of his head to the tip of his toes was one big ugly black burn. The doctors had coated his body with a blue liquid that made him look like some strange and terrible creature from another planet.

He was conscious and I was able to talk to him. He was only twenty-three years old and a teacher. He told me that he had to bear so many pressures coming from his family that in a moment of depression and despair he had gone out, doused himself with a liter of gasoline and set his body afire in the hope of ending it all. And now he lay dying in a hospital bed, his body one mass of toasted flesh.

That young man died a few hours later, the victim of his own inability to face harsh reality. He did not have to die. If only he had acquired that inner strength from which springs forth the courage to go on in the face of adversity, he would have survived. More than that, his trials and tribulations would have become instruments of personal growth instead of weapons for self-destruction.

You would be surprised if I told you that there are countless people who subconsciously want to die. Oh, they are not nearly as dramatic in their attempts as the young man above. However, they nevertheless wish to do away with themselves. Since they lack the courage to face harsh reality, they are also without the guts to commit suicide. Consequently, they merely float through life. They merely exist. They are not really ALIVE, they simply ARE.

Beryl Orris was correct when he wrote: "Without meaning there is an air of unreality about existence… the flight from reality becomes important to the degree that I cannot face and accept it."

YOU CAN'T RUN AWAY FROM YOURSELF

I KNOW A YOUNG lady who purposely changed her name because she said she didn't like the one her parents gave her at birth. I disagreed. I thought her real name was quite nice.

After probing more deeply into her life, I began to understand why this pretty woman didn't care to keep her baptismal name. It became obvious that, more than anything else, she disliked herself intensely and felt that by getting rid of her name, she was bidding goodbye to her past.

Of course, she was not really aware of all this. It was buried deep in her subconscious. But it was clear that by taking on a new name, she thought she could become a person other than herself.

However, it was a very simple matter indeed to break through the mask and see her little game for what it was. Just about the only person she was fooling was herself.

There are many people like this young lady who try to run away from themselves because they have such a terrible self-image. I have often said that the most difficult person I find to live with is me. Perhaps it is because I can never run away from myself. I can surely make all kinds of attempts to do so, however, ultimately, I am faced with the reality that is me. I can lie to myself a long time, but, in the end, I cannot run away from the truth and I will have to look at what I am and stop playing games with myself. People who do not have a high regard for themselves can never be successful because they don't have the self-confidence necessary to succeed in life. In fact, many people with a poor self-image are often driven by a strong inner force to destroy themselves morally and even physically.

One characteristic of the drug dependent, which is universal, is that he has a very low regard for himself. Perhaps that is why he does his best to do away with himself by abusing drugs.

There are, of course, many traits and characteristics that we need to correct and modify in our lives, but that is to be expected. We must not despair if we are not what we dream we should be. Remember that all of us are a mixture of strengths and weaknesses and that so long as we live, we remain such. The important thing is to eliminate as many weaknesses as possible and further build up our strong points.

We all have an abundance of goodness in us. We must not forget that when we feel down and depressed. Most of us must remember that we are very precious indeed. So much so, God was more than willing to die for us. And that is no little thing.

CONFRONT YOUR PROBLEMS

ONE OF THE GREATEST dangers to a successful marriage is the inability or the refusal on the part of one of those spouses to face a problem which is becoming a serious threat to their relationship. The danger becomes even greater when both husband and wife make a silent contract to ignore some trouble that could weaken and lessen their love for each other.

I am reminded of a pretty wife who refused to face the fact that her husband was playing around with other women. When she got word about his escapades from a number of impeccable sources, she confronted her husband, who was quick to deny it all. Instead of pursuing the matter to a more logical conclusion, the wife immediately broke off the discussion.

In spite of the repeated warnings of her closest friends, she insisted on dropping the matter there and then.

Well, to make a long story short, it was a rude awakening six months later when the parents of a young woman came to the house and accused the wife's husband of getting their daughter pregnant.

Then, the roof of that marriage caved in on both spouses. What else could you expect to happen when people run away from their problems? Unresolved problems have a way of catching up with people. Human beings can run fast, but problems have a tremendous staying power if they are not resolved. People run out of emotional breath. Problems don't.

Many of us are like the ostrich that buries its head in the sand whenever it finds itself in danger. We refuse to face the problem and try to resolve it. Instead, we quickly turn our backs and refuse to look. Some of us even stare at the problem straight in the eye and deny its very existence.

It's a little bit like a friend of mine who was deathly afraid of the dentist. He refused to visit the doctor until it came to a point when they had to extract all of his teeth. Or like another friend of mine who could not be convinced about the wisdom of seeing a doctor about a nagging pain in the stomach. He was afraid of what the findings would indicate. He thought it might be cancer. He didn't see the doctor in spite of his friend's urgings. Eight months later, he died of stomach cancer.

We all have problems. That's life. Nothing unusual about that. Besides, the good Lord gave us brains with which to resolve them. We can grow and mature if we learn to cope with our difficulties. We remain children emotionally when we run from our problems and refuse to even admit that they exist.

Bob Garon

When a man tries walking through life with his eyes closed, you can be sure that he is going to get hurt.

ACCEPT HARSH REALITY, BE HAPPY

WHY ARE PEOPLE unhappy? That's a loaded question. Yet, it's a question that I often ask myself. Perhaps it's because I see so many unhappy people.

Surely there are countless reasons people are unhappy, you will tell me. This man lost his wife in a fire. That woman's husband left her. This teenager cannot go to her class party tonight. That child's candy was stolen by a bigger boy.

People will give you reason after reason. However, the way I see it, people are basically unhappy because they allow themselves to be such. Why is it that this man is unhappy because he's poor and another man who is even poorer is very happy in his little rundown house? Here is a separated woman who is so miserable that she affects everybody within reach with her negativeness. Yet, just across the street lives another separated woman, the mother of seven children, who is relatively happy. Why is it that some kids in the DARE rehabilitation centers are very happy while others say they are miserable?

The reason is that the happy people in this world of ours are people who have come to terms with reality and with themselves.

An amputee who spends his whole life in a wheelchair is happier than most people and we wonder why. Shouldn't he be heart-broken? Shouldn't he be spending his time crying all over himself? The fact is that this disabled man has accepted the harsh reality in his life that he has lost his legs. And since he has come to terms with himself, he has no reason to be unhappy.

People who remain unhappy over an extended period of time are individuals who have no *acceptance*. They are not happy with life, people, conditions or hard realities. They have tried to change things to suit themselves, and have failed. Yet, they refuse to accept the inevitable.

I once met a woman who was still angry at God for "having taken my husband." The man died two years before. However, the wife still had not accepted the undeniable and real fact that her husband was dead and gone, never to return. She led a miserable life because she always talked "as if" he was present and did things the way "he would have wanted them done." Instead of redirecting her life accordingly, this woman insisted on living in a world of make-believe. Is it any wonder that she could not find happiness?

The next time you are unhappy, see if it isn't because either you refuse to accept the reality of a thing, person or situation or because you are having a tremendous difficulty adapting your life to something unpleasant.

If you don't want to remain unhappy, there is no reason you should. All you have to do is live with yourself and with reality as harmoniously as possible.

However, if you insist on being unhappy by refusing to have anything to do with harsh reality, then of course, even God and all the saints in heaven cannot stop you. Be unhappy, and enjoy it!

ACCEPTANCE IS NOT FATALISM

ONE OF THE MOST important factors in leading a happy Christian life is *acceptance*. Even if a person is not God-oriented; even if he doesn't believe in the existence of God, he must have acceptance if he is to be happy.

People are often mistaken in their idea of acceptance. They think that to have acceptance means to be lazy and to sit back and wait for whatever "God sends us." Many think of acceptance as a form of fatalism. It's far from that.

The mature man, the solid Christian, isn't lazy. He doesn't stand around and wait for God to spoon-feed him. On the contrary, the mature person is dynamic, moving, and exciting.

He does his best to make things happen in his life and in the lives of those around him. He works hard at planning, organizing, and executing. He is a firm believer in the old maxim: "God helps those who help themselves."

The man who has a deep acceptance works hard, as if there were no God in his life. Then, when he has done his very best, he prays hard, as if it's all up to God.

He understands that it is childish to expect God to "baby" him all his life. He knows that inner growth depends, to a large extent, on the personal motivations of a man.

The mature person fully realizes that things cannot always go his way. He has outgrown his childish ways. He does not expect to cat lollipops all his life. He has learned that life is a combination of bitter-sweet and that hard times are unavoidable.

When difficult days come upon him, he doesn't break and run. He knows that this is only a passing pain which will heal, given the time. He remains calm under stress and accepts it as a part of the game of life.

He still works hard to change things. Although he accepts the present state of affairs as a reality in his life, he may not be satisfied with things and will do anything and everything to change them. Meanwhile, he calmly moves on towards his goals.

He who has little or no acceptance reacts quite differently. He feels deep frustration because he doesn't get his way. He wastes lots of time wishing that things would be different. But they're never different.

He gets angry at the Lord and the world because he just refuses to accept the realities in his life. He ends up a bitter and frustrated man.

We all run into stone walls every now and then. We all have to face disappointments, whether we like it or not. What makes the difference and determines whether or not we will make the best of what we have is acceptance. That's what life is all about- God or no God.

SO YOU HAVE A PROBLEM

DO YOU HAVE A problem? You do? Well, that's good. It's good because if you know how to deal with your problem, it could be a tremendous opportunity for growth and success.

There was a time in my life when I was scared to death of encountering problems. The mere thought of having to struggle with a problem would depress me. In other words, I worried about problems even before they came into my life.

I think that many of us are like that. We get ulcers over things that "might be" but "never are." We imagine all kinds of problems that never materialize. We are so anxious about what the future might bring, even if we have all the reasons to hope for a brighter to tomorrow. In short, we are often prophets of doom.

Everyone has problems. We all know that. However, even if we know it, we sometimes refuse to accept this obvious reality. It is one thing to know, but to accept is something altogether different. Although we are all aware that life without problems is an impossibility, we nevertheless try to pretend that we might just get away with encountering them if we are lucky enough. This is nonsense. Or there are times when we exaggerate our problems. We see them as being much larger than they are in reality.

If only we could get the right perspective and put problems in their proper focus, then perhaps we would not worry as much about them. If we only understood that every real achievement in life is due to a great extent to a problem that a man had to face in the past, then perhaps we would not be so terrified of them. All progress is a result of problems that were solved.

Problems force a man to think. More than that, they compel him to think in a positive and creative way. They push him toward new unexplored avenues. If a man is to find a solution (and very often, he has no other choice), then he is put into a situation that calls for imaginative problem-solving.

The most successful men are people who have had more than their fair share of problems. What made them effectively climb the ladder to success was not so much the problems they encountered, but the way they were able to solve them. They needed a positive mental attitude.

The successful people in our midst are individuals who are effective "problem solvers." They, of course, do not enjoy having problems, but they fully understand that there can be no success without the corresponding problems that accompany it. And because they realize that this is a reality that cannot be swept under the rug, they are better equipped with healthy positive thinking to meet their problems head-on. They don't dodge them. And because they do not avoid them, they get used to dealing with them. They become more at ease with conflict and they are able to absorb more of it than most people. This accounts for their success.

The next time you run into a problem, you can do one of two things. See it as an unfortunate curse in your life or look at it as an opportunity for growth. The choice you make will spell the difference between success and failure.

EMOTIONAL PIMPLES IN LIFE

THIS CHAPTER IS all about pimples. Ever watch a teener stand before the mirror and worry about those pimples that keep surfacing just often enough to scar that smooth complexion every youngster dreams of having? Would you believe that many people (some of them way past their teens) get thoroughly upset by pimples?

Even the pretty woman lives in fear that one morning she may wake up to find an ugly pimple rearing its head on the side of her nose. And when it does happen, it's as if half the world had fallen in on her. She spends a lot of time looking for ways to camouflage her pimple, distract from it, or destroy it outright. Although she is pretty all over, she focuses on that solitary pimple sitting quietly alongside her nose. The truth of the matter is that she exaggerates its importance out of all proportion.

All of us have pimples, emotional pimples. None is exempt from those nagging little problems that put us down. How often have we focused far too much time and attention on minute problems and allowed them to depress us?

People are unhappy because they let themselves fall into the depths of depression and despair. We all have problems. Some are big; most are small. Some deserve lots of time and concentration; most call for nothing more than a shrug. Yet, we never learn to deal properly with the emotional pimples in our lives.

We let insignificant events be magnified by our fertile imagination. We do nothing to resist that dreaded killer of men, self-pity. And self-pity has a way of putting emphasis on the negative, no matter what its size, shape, or color.

If you leave a pimple alone, it will go away more quickly than if you keep playing with it. It's the same with lots of the emotional pimples (those minor irritants) we encounter in life. If we could only shrug them off and ignore them as the unimportant happenings they are, they too would go away.

I'm not talking about the deep wounds we often have to deal with. They have to be attended to immediately. I mean the pimples, the little things that we allow to upset us and that get out of hand.

Knowing what's important and what isn't is all part of growing up. I can understand why big problems get people down. However, many of us fall even when we are pushed lightly. We do what boxers who "throw fights" do; we "take a dive" and lose battles that are within easy grasp of victory.

It has often and correctly been said that life is a never-ending series of battles that must be fought relentlessly. The tough fights are hard to win. We shouldn't lose the easy ones. A pimple should be treated like a pimple and not be given undue attention.

GETTING ALONG WITH PEOPLE

THERE ARE TIMES when we get so disgusted with people that we wonder why God made them in the first place. It isn't because we have lost faith in humans. Rather, it's just because some persons are so difficult to deal with that they make our lives miserable.

I'm sure all of us have felt this way at some time or other in our lives. We often bump into people who are so mad at the world and themselves that we wonder how they can get along with anybody.

What many of us fail to understand is that, for the most part, we *allow ourselves* to be troubled by difficult people. We *let* them get on our nerves. The greater part of the problem lies within our own selves.

If you want to get along with difficult people, here are a few points you would do well to ponder.

Don't think they must apologize to you. Recognize the wisdom of overlooking the hurt caused you in the hope that a better atmosphere will be created.

Don't think they *must* admit that they are wrong. Recognize how unlikely this is to happen. Meanwhile, you are not getting anywhere or making any progress.

Concentrate on doing what is best and fair for all concerned.

Don't think that it is necessarily all their fault. Recognize that the fault could be partly yours. It could be your attitude, or manner, or method of approach.

Don't think that they are being difficult just to annoy you and to spite you. Understand that difficult people are so usually because of tremendous inner conflicts. Besides, they are difficult the world over and difficult to everybody. Keep your "cool" and try to take it all in stride.

Don't think they are not worth bothering with and don't be rude to them. Realize instead the common sense of discouraging bad feelings and encouraging a "truce," even though you may never be able to like one another.

Don't think they are going around turning other people against you. Tell yourself that this may not be true and give them the benefit of the doubt. Make sure that a few of your good friends know the real facts.

Don't think of them as your enemies for life. Understand that they might have been influenced and prejudiced against you. Perhaps their minds have been poisoned by others. Once they know the truth about you, their attitude could change. They just might become great friends of yours someday.

Don't think about them all the time and allow them to make you unhappy. Check out your own attitudes. Be sure that you have done all you could do. Then stop worrying and forget it. Let time work it out. Take it easy.

GROWTH CALLS FOR SHARING

THERE ARE MANY reasons for the communication gap that exists between people. But perhaps the greatest single factor is fear.

We are afraid to speak up because we fear rejection and hostility. We remain silent because we worry (fear) about how our statements will be received. We retreat into ourselves and hide our innermost thoughts from those we should be sharing with because we fear betrayal.

If a person does not have confidence in himself and cannot look at himself in a favorable light, he will fear authentic and deep level communication. He will live in dread of being discovered for what he really is. Afraid to be known, he will spend most of his time building formidable defenses in order to keep people from penetrating his real self too deeply.

How often I have come across sweethearts and married couple who have been keeping secrets that serve to eat away at their insides. If only they could share them, they would be liberated. But fear locks them firmly in the solitary confinement of themselves and immobilizes them for years and sometimes for a lifetime.

What is the remedy? Among other things, what is of prime importance is *trust.* We must take risks in order to gain anything of value. Sometimes the gamble does not work out; sometimes it pays big dividends. You can't win every time. We all know this, yet not everybody can accept it as a reality in their lives.

Whenever we do invest in others and open our hearts to them, we are taking chances. We just might get hurt by people we thought were well-meaning. Often, we do. When that happens, we usually feel like closing up the shop and going home. We do not want to be hurt anymore.

But what other choice do we have except to open up and try again? And again, if necessary. Our growth and salvation lie in sharing and not in hoarding. Those who refuse to share to die a slow death from emotional stagnation. Their friendships remain on a superficial level and they can never seem to cultivate satisfying and rewarding relationships with people.

Sharing is a risky business. There is no question about it. However, there is no other acceptable alternative if one is to grow steadily and lead a happy and successful life.

HOW TO DEAL WITH LONELINESS

THERE ARE MOMENTS in a man's life when the sun is suddenly obscured and storm clouds gather on the horizon. There are times when everything seems to go wrong. The dry season has set into a man's heart and where there was once lush greenery, there is now only dust and withering leaves turned a dull brown. He feels pushed into the corner by his enemies and abandoned by his friends.

His faith in God is shaken. And perhaps, worst of all, he feels deep and painful loneliness which cuts into his heart and causes him indescribable anguish. He sees his dreams fade into nothingness and does not have the emotional strength to dream new ones. It seems that all the positiveness in his life has suddenly vanished, almost without a trace. He has nobody to turn to since his "friends" are nowhere to be found.

It is in times like these that the saving factor must be either a strong faith in God or in someone who will move in quickly and be a positive force for renewal. There is a desperate need for renewal. There is a desperate need for a "bridge" over troubled water. Whether it be constructed of steel, wood or rope, there is nevertheless a need for some safety from turbulent waters below.

In other words, what is needed is a measure of peace, cessation of conflict. That is why it is of utmost importance that someone comes into the picture who will serve to instill calm. Someone who will inspire trust and confidence. Someone who can create an emotional climate that is conducive to openness and sharing.

When a man is down, lonely and beaten, he needs to hear kind words of encouragement. Because of his tendency to wallow in self-pity, he needs to be assured that he is still very much wanted and highly regarded by his peers. It is imperative that he feels accepted and loved. He must be convinced of his own self-worth.

We all fall into the depths of discouragement and even despair at one time or another in our lives. Nothing unusual about this. I have yet to meet a mature person who has never felt the pangs of loneliness which come with the pain of rejection. This is an integral part of the human condition, which cannot be avoided.

If only we can show enough intelligence to recognize loneliness when it makes its appearance in our lives and if we are humble and mature enough to ask for help in dealing with it, then it becomes an experience which can aid us to grow tremendously. It is not loneliness which kills the human spirit. It is the inability to deal with it properly that destroys the heart of man.

LONELINESS IS ALSO A BLESSING

EACH OF US HAS been alone. We have all, at one time or another, been starved for companionship. Each of us has ended days, weeks, months, perhaps even years without finding a meaningful relationship that could relieve us from the loneliness that was slowly eating away at our insides. We had to admit to ourselves at some point in our lives that we were lonely and afraid.

I remember my long walks to and from school. I remember how my heart cried out for a friend with whom I could share my innermost thoughts and feelings. I remember the countless times since my boyhood when I felt the same pangs of loneliness.

However, I'm not sad about all that. In many ways, loneliness is a blessing. It can have a sobering effect on a man. Loneliness has a way of causing a man to realize things that would otherwise go unnoticed in his life.

The experience of loneliness gives a person a new appreciation of things and people he had perhaps taken for granted. Did you know that water has a distinct taste and flavor? Try going without any liquid for a whole day and then slowly sip a glass of cold water. You will discover, as I have, that water is the finest tasting drink in the world.

In the same way, a man who has experienced deep loneliness is in a stronger position to enjoy that tremendous feeling of exhilaration that comes about with love. He is more sensitive and more appreciative of the blessings that friendship brings.

When a man has been up the whole night, he becomes very much aware of the slightest trace of light that signifies the dawning of a new day.

When a man has gone without love and deep friendship for some time, it takes just a little bit of tender loving care to cause him to feel deeply what others might take for granted.

Lonely people are easy targets for insincere persons who are alert enough to understand how a little love and affection can have such a tremendous impact on the one who feels that he is living in a world without love.

A man who has experienced crippling loneliness fully realizes the beauty of love and the value of friendship. He treasures every tender moment that his faithful friend offers him because he is reminded of the total isolation and the tremendous suffering that almost destroyed him emotionally.

In time of deep loneliness and great suffering, the value and meaning of life are re-examined. The lone survivor drifting on a tiny rubber raft on the Pacific Ocean, the man lost in the jungle, the mother slowly dying of cancer and the prisoner in death row: all of them feel deep loneliness.

The lonely man tends to review his life. He remembers the bitterness of the past and how it need not have been. He recalls those moments of intense loving and deep sharing and wishes that they could have been more numerous and longer lasting. He becomes aware of the incidents of petty dishonesty in his life and suddenly realizes how silly and useless they were. He remembers the hurt he caused other people and feels he would very much like to make up for his cruelty by whispering a few loving words to the offended parties.

The lonely and isolated man searches for answers to life. He looks for a better life. He is willing to sacrifice many things and even his whole self in order to attain some sort of union with somebody in order to drive away from his life the feeling of loneliness that is slowly pushing him to the edge of madness.

Perhaps for the first time in his life, he becomes honest in facing conflicts and problems. He longs to validate his values and priorities in order to reassure himself that he has done right and is on the correct path.

The lonely man seeks deliverance. He yearns to break out of his cell and reach out to the world. He searches for the companionship of another human being and when he cannot find this union, he often is forced to look somewhere else for relief.

It is indeed amazing how often, in times such as these, that a man bumps into God.

IT'S THE MAN WHO HATES WHO SUFFERS

AN AMERICAN COLUMNIST, Sydney Harris, once wrote a story about an incident that happened when he was accompanying his friend to a newsstand. The friend greeted the newspaper seller very courteously, but in return received gruff and discourteous service. Accepting the newspaper, which was impolitely pushed at him, the friend of Harris smiled and wished the seller a nice day. As the two friends walked down the street, the columnist asked:

"Does he always treat you so rudely? And are you always so polite and friendly to him?"

"Yes, I am."

"Why are you so nice to him when he is so unfriendly to you?"

"Because I don't want him to decide how I'm going to act."

`This story got me thinking about how we allow people and things to make us unhappy. I remember what my Dad once said to me when I told him how much I hated so-and-so.

"Bobby," he said, "I don't want you to hate anybody, because when you hate somebody, you're unhappy and I want you to be happy always."

He was right. We so often let people upset us. They say nasty things and we fly into a rage and fight back as our blood pressure slowly rises. We allow people to embarrass us and make us sad.

I'm like that too. I think we all are. However, it doesn't mean that just because we have always been this way that we should allow things to go on without some striving to change the situation.

The solid man, the mature person, is one who can take a terrific beating (verbally or emotionally) and still survive nicely; he is one who does not bend with every attack on his feelings; he is never broken by unjust criticism and the remarks of the jealous and the envious.

In other words, he is in good control of his feelings. If he is hurt, he knows his mind should move into the picture and take over because he is intelligent enough to know that *feelings don't think*.

Whenever I bump into people who are very nasty and aggressive and who come at me with vicious verbal attacks, I force my feelings to retreat and give away to my thinking. I try to look on these people as *sick*. And there are many sick people in our midst. There are a tremendous number of persons in our society who are in desperate need of psychological help. They are not mad, but emotionally unbalanced. They have their prejudices and pettiness; they feel defensive because they are threatened; they hurt people because they are insecure and feel secured.

I don't always succeed, but I do try, like the friend of Harris, *not* to allow people to determine my blood pressure.

FIGHTING HATRED WITH LOVE

THIS IS A CHAPTER for those of you readers who have an enemy and would like to torture him. If there is somebody in your life who hates you with an intense hatred and is making your day miserable, then perhaps you would be interested in knowing how you could reciprocate and cause him countless uneasy moments. If you don't have an enemy in the world, then don't waste your time reading this page. I am only interested in helping people fight their enemies in the most effective way.

If you have an enemy, I suggest you kill him. Kill him with love, that is. No, I'm not kidding. Neither am I trying to be a smart guy. I am merely suggesting to you a tried and tested method that has worked over and over down through the ages.

If a man hates you, he will somehow exhibit some form of hostility towards you. He will surely strike at you either directly or indirectly. He will hurt you with his own hands, or he will try to reach you by going through others.

It doesn't really matter how he hurts you because any method he uses is going to cause you a considerable amount of pain. Your normal and natural reaction, of course, will be to retaliate by hurting him right back. This is quite understandable, and I suppose nobody can really blame you for doing your best to chop his head off.

But don't be surprised if you lose your own head in the process. You can't expect him to stand there and take his punishment. He will, of course, fight back and before you know it, round two is underway. Some people fight hundreds of rounds with an enemy. They throw countless punches at each other. And yet nobody seems to win. The reason for this is quite clear. Hatred breeds only more hatred; hostility, more hostility, and so on until somebody really and truly dies. When this happens, the winning party can celebrate only a very shallow victory. If the man had not died, he would still be fighting with gusto. So, I suppose his death didn't really prove anything.

Why not try fighting hatred and hostility with love? I remember reading somewhere in a book by Theodore Reik that the command of Jesus Christ to love one's enemy is in fact a very effective way of destroying one's enemies. Putting it simply, it all boils down to this: How do you think a big bully feels when he is beating up a little guy who refuses to fight back and only smiles at him? In reality, he is getting angrier by the minute because his enemy smiles at him and calls him brother. Ever try hitting a blank wall? If you have not yet tried it, then please do. It will give you an idea of what it feels like to hit a man who refuses to fight back.

When you refuse to fight hatred with hatred, you are in effect causing your enemy to lay down his arms. Unless a man is mentally disturbed, he cannot enjoy continuing his attacks on someone who blesses him. He will, in effect, feel awfully cheap about the whole thing.

Remember that hating is really a game that people play, and, like all games, it takes at least two people to play it. If you insist on getting out and refusing to play any longer, then what can your enemy do? Oh, I suppose he can listen to his curses bounce off the wall and come back to him. He can repeat the same insults over and over again, hoping that they will somehow hurt you. However, when he gets absolutely no response from you, except perhaps a blessing, he will see the ridiculousness of the whole situation and cease making war. If you don't believe me, try it. It really works.

ON HEATED ARGUMENTS

Have you ever thought about those little arguments you have had with a friend which ended up becoming veritable screaming matches? Have you wondered how such insignificant irritants could have been blown up all out of proportion?

Let's face it. Arguments among friends, sweethearts and spouses can be so destructive that they are capable of causing untold damage to a relationship. What is sad is that things need not be so.

I read somewhere that, in an argument, "all is said during the first five minutes." After that, there is only a series of repetitions that become longer and more vicious each time the two parties run over the same ground.

I believe there is a lot of truth to that. Usually, what is said in the first minutes of an argument and how it is said will set the tone for the rest of the discussion. If two people begin yelling at each other, chances are that they will go on screaming no matter how reasonable their positions are.

Arguments have a way of escalating out of control. Unless they are carefully watched by one or both parties, they can bring terrible destruction on a healthy relationship. They have been known to quickly sound the death knell of long-standing friendships. They have provoked men to such anger that they have killed to settle them.

I am a man who likes to talk. I enjoy discussion. I also sometimes get into arguments. And since I have a short temper, which I have been working hard to control all my life, hot arguments are no strangers to me. I am not proud of my outbursts because I happen to believe that they are a sign of weaknesses. I am proud, though, of the fact that I have been trying ways and means to prevent them from doing too much harm to myself and to those who surround me.

Perhaps the reason why I am writing these lines is to share with those of you who have a similar problem, a gimmick that I have found to be most helpful to me. Whenever I can perceive an argument beginning to get out of hand, I set forth my position as briefly and as unemotionally as possible. If my friend cannot get my message or is getting angry precisely because he has understood it, then I will break off the fight and retreat like a genuine coward. I will refuse to fuel the fires of his anger by continuing the discussion when it is clear that tension and frustration is building up to fever pitch. Like what was written above, if after a few minutes, the basic points have been set forth and there seems to be no real progress, then breaking off the argument seems to me to be the better part of wisdom.

The cooling-off period can do wonders. If the matter is unimportant, it should not be brought up again and is better left alone and unattended to. If it is of concern, then you can be sure it will be taken up once more. Only this time, there may be more thought and less feeling behind the discussion.

STICKING TO THE POINT

WHENEVER TWO people in love argue, they usually make one tragic mistake. They hardly ever stick to the point.

Take the case of Jun and Virgie. They have been married for five years. They have three children and are very much in love. However, Jun has been coming home late these past few months, and this has given rise to countless, senseless arguments. I use the word "senseless" because nobody ever ends up the winner.

Whenever Virgie attempts to find out why her husband is late, Jun accuses her of nagging him. And whenever she insists, he says that had he known that she would be like this, he would "never have married her."

This type of exchange usually accomplishes only one thing. It serves to widen the gap between people. Argumentation, like the public debate, is an art. Not just anybody can argue intelligently and effectively. It takes someone who can really understand its fine points. The reason people get hurt during an argument is that they do not stick to the point.

In any kind of discussion, keeping the point at issue in focus at all times is of prime importance. The moment a person moves away from the question at hand, you can be sure that there will be trouble. It often happens that after two hours of heated words, two people end up not knowing what the argument was all about. So many issues were brought into the picture that the reason for the discussion was lost in the heated exchange of words.

I suppose that the cause of all the confusion usually lies in the frantic attempts of one or both parties to defend. When a man knows that he is weak at this point, he attempts to divert the attention of the person who is probing his weakness. So. if a guy is staying out late because there is someone else in his life, he can't very well talk about his "outings" without being discovered, so he accuses his wife, rightly or wrongly, of being a nagger. In this way, he succeeds in avoiding the issue by bringing up the question of nagging.

Another way of defending oneself and drawing attention away from the issue is to go to the attack. The wife accuses him of being a drunkard. He turns around and tells her that she was not a virgin when he married her.

The loss of virginity 26 years ago has nothing to do with the issue of his being a drunkard at the present time. But the guy knows that by scraping at the old wound, he will draw her attention away from his own weak point, thereby protecting himself from further probing.

These tactics never solve anything, and when used, they usually make matters worse. In fact, they only serve to frustrate because, in spite of all the arguments, no progress is ever made. So even the sincerest person begins to have second thoughts about the usefulness of talking.

If you are going to argue with someone (wife, friend, sweetheart) be sure that you are not faked out by divisive tactics. Stick to the point. You will prevent a little grass fire from turning into a raging blaze.

However, if you have a solid argument and you feel sure that your "loving opponent" is wrong and knows it, then expect the usual smoke screen, especially if the other person is not the humblest individual in the world.

Another thing to remember if you are going to have an effective discussion without hurting needlessly is this: the less emotion, the better. The moment people get emotional, thinking becomes difficult and sometimes ceases altogether.

In fact, when a person becomes so upset that he begins to throw around emotionally charged accusations, then you can be sure that almost all rational discussion is about to end.

The important thing to remember about an argument is that personalities should not enter into the picture, unless, of course, the issue is one of personality.

You can tell him what you do not like *about* him, but you must continuously reassure him that you still love *him*. If you do not really care for a person, then everybody expects personal attacks. But this anger does not have any place in intelligent argumentation.

The next time you must talk things over with someone you love, in order not to cause undue hurt feelings, I advise you to first establish what the issue is.

ON ENVY AND JEALOUSY

ENVY AND JEALOUSY are perhaps the ugliest defects a person can possess. When a man behaves in a childish way, we pity him since he is only retarding his own emotional growth. The woman who is forever losing her temper is really angry at herself deep down inside. And the lazy guy who refuses to do anything is only hurting himself by not developing his potential.

However, the envious man and the jealous woman are others-oriented. You can be sure that a lot of people are going to get hurt (and some badly) when a jealous female goes on the warpath. And when an envious colleague begins planning the destruction of a rival, you had better clear the deck and expect lots of dirty moves.

Envy is a natural feeling that rushes to the surface almost automatically in the lives of insecure and unfulfilled people. And since we are all insecure and uneasy with ourselves to a greater or lesser degree, all of us have experienced that strange feeling of emotional pain and envy.

I have been envious of people I believed were superior to me many times. I admit it. I am not proud of it, but I don't think you would believe me if I told you otherwise. Neither can you expect me to believe you if you tell me that you were never jealous and envious.

These feelings are realities in our lives. Because we are human beings, feelings are an integral part of our lives and they come floating into sight almost imperceptibly. We don't really ask for most of the feelings that we experience. They just pop into our lives without permission. Once they are present, it is up to us to decide whether or not to "act off our feelings" or to control them.

We "act off" feelings when we follow their dictates blindly without thinking of the consequences of our actions.

Dealing with our feelings of jealousy and envy is not all that simple. It calls for a strong and disciplined mind, and a noble one too. When I feel jealous of the good fortune of others, it takes a real effort of the will to fight off these feelings. It means striving hard to reason out things in a way that I will come to understand that I am not at all in such a poor situation myself and that I have many blessings to count.

Some people hide behind their feelings and justify their talk and behavior by excusing themselves with the phrase "...but that's the way I feel." There is no mistaking their feelings. That's not news. However, feelings don't necessarily justify behavior.

It takes a lifetime to learn how to control our feelings. It takes that long because total maturity is impossible for us. Complete maturity presupposes full mastery over our feelings. This is something none of us is capable of achieving. Nevertheless, it is in the interest of a happier life that we should do everything in our power to become the masters of those unpredictable and potentially destructive negative feelings that seem to be constantly moving into our lives without invitation. It's not easy, but the least we can do is try.

BE HAPPY WITH WHAT YOU HAVE

WHY IS IT that so many of us are so unhappy so often? I suppose there are many reasons. But I believe that envy lies at the heart of most of our unhappiness.

Unhappy people are discontented people. It doesn't matter if you live in a beautiful home or in a nipa hut. It makes no difference if you are very intelligent or extremely limited. If you are disconnected, you are going to be very unhappy.

And if you stop and think a moment about discontentment, you will soon understand that there is always at least a touch of envy present. Envious people never seem to be satisfied with what they have. They are constantly looking over the fence into the other guy's backyard. They always seem to find that the grass is greener there. So much so, that they miss the beauty that is right there before them.

I believe that all of us feel envious at one time or another. I am a very outgoing person. Some people envy me for that. But I cannot play a musical instrument or sing very well. I envy others for that. I envy people who are good with numbers (I constantly flunked my math). My classmates, on the other hand, envied me for my very high marks in history.

And that's how it goes throughout life. We are constantly comparing ourselves, our situation in life, and our fortune or misfortune with that of other people. We want everything. We desire to be number one in all categories. And when we come out second or third or tenth, we are very unhappy about the whole thing. In fact, we become so discontented that we cannot seem to enjoy second or third or tenth place.

Envy does strange things to a person. It denies him the right to enjoy what he has. Because envy draws a man into the never-never world of dreamland, the envious individual is unable to enjoy the here-and-now.

No matter how much you have, if you are plagued with envy, you will never have enough. You will be incapable of enjoying what you have, be it little or a lot, because you can never feel satisfaction with what you have. You will chase after rainbows all your life and never find that pot of gold that you are so desperately seeking.

Enjoy life. Dream if you must. But be content with what you have until your dreams become a reality. Understand that you can not have everything. And if you did, you would be bored because there would be nothing left to strive for. Do not compare yourself with anyone because that would be unfair. There is a uniqueness about you which cannot be compared with any other human. You are not superior or inferior to others. You are merely different. You are you. Work at becoming a better you. Be satisfied with that and you will enjoy happiness and peace of soul you never dreamt possible in this life.

UNREALISTIC EXPECTATION

THERE IS ONE reality that friends, lovers and married people have difficulty accepting. That is that two people rarely have the capacity to satisfy all the needs of each other for a lifetime. It is so hard for a wife to admit that she is inadequate when it concerns the needs of the man she loves. It is undoubtedly very painful to face the fact that her husband will have to go elsewhere to fulfill some of his needs; that she cannot possibly be the answer to all his wants.

It is natural to desire to possess a loved one so completely and that he becomes totally dependent. I said it is "natural"; that does not mean it is a good thing. Let's be honest. An individual's needs, even only one person's, are so many and varied that one cannot ever be expected to answer all of them. This is just simply impossible. Thus, it is unrealistic to expect one's partner in marriage or a sweetheart to fulfill all our needs.

Many have relationships that end up on the rocks because of unrealistically high expectations that could never, even under the best circumstances, be realized. Young lovers, starry-eyed and blind to much of reality, who get into love and marriage expecting that they will be all to each other, are in for a rude awakening. They soon discover that nobody has a monopoly on good things; that God has spread His blessings all around the place so that we will be encouraged to interact with as many people as possible; and that unless they are willing to allow each other the freedom to seek additional fulfillment elsewhere, conflict will soon arise.

Watching a loved one go off to seek growth and satisfaction (I don't mean sexual satisfaction) that he believes is essential for his development is tough on anybody in love. It is unbearable for the person who is deeply insecure. The wife who feels that her marriage is shaky can experience only fear and apprehension when she sees her husband looking elsewhere to satisfy an important need. For example, if a plain and simple woman is married to a scientist, she will soon come to understand that her man has a need to interact with others who have the same interests. The need is less if she can understand his work and converse with him about it. Otherwise, she will have to give way and encourage him to seek out people who are familiar with the projects that are so important to him.

It takes humility, a feeling of genuine security and an authentic concern for the growth of the loved one to admit that you cannot answer to all of his needs. If you can admit this, sincerely and truly, chances are that your love is healthy. If not, I suggest you re-examine your relationship. It most likely is in need of some strengthening.

DON'T EXPECT TOO MUCH

IF PEOPLE ARE sad, unhappy and unfulfilled, it is because they seem unable to draw satisfaction from their lives. So many of us succumb to the temptation of wishing that we were something or someone that we are not.

We hear melodious sounds of a well-known singer and we envy him for his voice. We think that if we could only produce sounds such as these, then we would gain great happiness and deep satisfaction. Then, we hear a great public speaker. We dream and fantasize about how fulfilled we would be if only we had the ability to communicate our ideas the way he does. We meet a learned man and think that if only we had the vast store of knowledge that is in his head, we would indeed gain great happiness. And if only we could shoot baskets like Bobby Jaworski, we would gain acceptance and popularity, which would surely afford us more joy in life.

People who have unrealistic expectations about themselves can never be happy. They can never be happy because they adhere to the illogical idea that one should be thoroughly competent, adequate, intelligent, and achieving in all possible aspects. Thinking in this manner is unreal. It will inevitably lead to failure and frustration. You cannot be a star in everything you do. It is impossible to be number one all the time. Even the greatest basketball team has points scored against it. Mohammed Ali gets hit on the nose many times during his fights; and even victorious armies lose battles.

Why is it that people want to be tops in everything they do? Is it an inner drive for excellence? I am not sure. Perhaps it is envy and excessive pride. A young man once told me he would never rest until he was first in all his undertakings. I replied that he would remain restless, unsatisfied, and unfulfilled all his life.

Now, don't get me wrong. I am not saying that one should be satisfied with mediocrity. Surely the striving for excellence should always be foremost in a man's mind. But that is not my point. Of course, a man should always do his very best in everything that he attempts in life. However, he cannot possibly expect to be a winner all the time. His realistic outlook on life has taught him that even those who give their best come out second, fifth, and perhaps even last. He sees life a little bit like the Olympics games. The glory lies not so much in winning but in participating and giving the best that one has to offer. That is the heart of the matter.

This, however, presupposes that one sees himself as an imperfect creature who is limited by a number of specific -weaknesses. In order to do this, one must possess a healthy amount of humility as well as insight. It is not easy to admit that one cannot draw a straight line or sing two consecutive notes or speak very well in public. We all know how difficult it is to admit that one is not always a winner. We realize how hard it is to acknowledge the superiority of one's peers. It is easy for a winner to congratulate a loser. It is more difficult for the loser to sincerely recognize the fact that he is second best.

Yet, unless we learn to do this graciously and sincerely, we will never gain peace of mind. We will forever be indulging in useless fantasy and destructive daydreams. If, on the other hand, somehow, someday, we learn to see ourselves as we are, then we will recognize our rightful place among our peers. This will go a long way in helping us to appreciate ourselves the way God meant it to be.

AMBIVALENT FEELINGS

The circumstances of life inevitably involve stress and tension. I have said this many times. Perhaps the reason I have repeated it so often is that most people do not realize that their happiness will be determined largely by the way they cope with the stress. The inability to deal effectively with stressful situations will surely spell trouble and lots of unhappiness.

Stress develops because our objectives in life and our needs are not always easily satisfied. We set goals. When we cannot attain them, we get frustrated. People react to frustrations in many different ways. Those who are unable to effectively deal with frustrations find themselves constantly knocking their heads against the wall. Frustration occurs when we cannot get what we want.

A major source of frustration is conflict between two opposing desires. A man is in love and wants to marry his sweetheart. His parents do not like the woman and threaten to cut off all financial aid if he goes ahead with his plans to marry. The young man is not yet financially stable and needs the support of his parents. He sees marriage as a desirable goal. However, he perceives the financial help that his parents can give him as also desirable. Conflict is born.

Conflict may also arise when there is only one desired goal involved, but many approaches to that goal. A young man may be free to marry and have all the necessary financial and moral support. If, however, he cannot make up his mind which of three women to marry, then he is in a state of conflict.

What makes conflict so difficult to deal with is that it usually involves goals that are at once desirable and undesirable. I like sweets, but I like to keep a slim waistline. A woman falls in love with a man. That's wonderful. The only problem is that he is married.

The attitude towards a goal at once wanted and disliked is what psychologists call an ambivalent attitude. Ambivalent attitudes are very common. A teenager runs away from home because he feels stifled by his dominating parents. A few weeks later, he returns home because he needs their support and protection. His attitude towards his parents is ambivalent. A wife has intense feelings of hostility towards her husband because he is having an affair with another woman. At the same time, she loves him deeply. Her feelings towards her husband are ambivalent.

It is the kind of ambivalence that causes us so much anxiety. We often lose sleep over it. We don't know whether to go ahead or to retreat. We weigh the pros and cons over and over again. We just cannot seem to decide what to do.

It is this seeming inability to make a decision that causes us so much anguish. Day after day, week after week, we are kept hanging as it were by this constant vacillation. We seem to be getting nowhere and we are suffering as we run around in circles.

The only way to relieve this kind of pain is to resolve the conflict. However, before this can be done, one must be aware of the nature, the cause of the conflict. Often, it's not as easy as it seems. One may have to spend a considerable amount of time talking to a wise counselor. However, when a man has done his best to investigate his situation as thoroughly as possible, then he must decide to move in one direction or another. Decision-making is of utmost importance. If a man knows in his mind what he must do but cannot muster the courage to do it, then his frustration is simply increased by the knowledge that he has an answer within reach but cannot seem to move. Making the wrong decision can mean much pain. Not making any decision at all, one way or the other way, can cause a whole lot more hurt.

After you have spent a reasonable amount of time thinking about a problem, decide on a course of action. Once you have decided, move. You will be surprised how often you will do the right thing.

HOW TO WIPE OUT GUILTY FEELINGS

WHY IS IT that so many people refuse to believe that there is a spark of greatness in them? Why do countless individuals think so little of themselves and spend their time knocking themselves down in the eyes of others? Why so little self-esteem and so much emotional self-destruction?

I suppose there are many factors that account for all these. However, I believe that guilt feelings are a major cause of emotional problems. Feelings of guilt eat away at a man's insides like an emotional cancer and let him die a slow and agonizing death. They cause his personality to erode.

The child who steals away money from his dad's pocket is plagued with guilt feelings. He no longer feels comfortable in his father's presence. Although his parents are unaware of his theft, he is aware of it and his guilt torments him. The youngster whose mother died while giving birth to him is burdened with tremendous guilt when told that he caused his mom's death. Even if he had no objective or subjective guilt, he may carry false guilt feelings within himself all the days of his life.

The husband who has been unfaithful to his wife cannot feel comfortable in her presence anymore. She feels it; he feels it. Things are not the same anymore.

The man who purposely transgresses the law of God is also visited with guilt feelings. If he doesn't believe in God, he may feel it less or not at all. If he is a God-fearing individual, he feels uncomfortable until he is able to clean himself up. We Christians have all felt this at one time or another in our lives.

How do we wipe out these guilt feelings that drag us down so deeply? I suppose it depends on the guilt. A sincere confession can do it when it comes to our relationship with the Almighty. In our dealings with others, I have always thought that the best way is to be open and frank about our guilt. A person has to share his secret guilts with someone in order to be freed from them. He must talk about them, preferably to the offended party. When forgiveness has been granted, the burden of the guilt is greatly reduced if not completely wiped out. If there is no forgiveness forthcoming, one can at least be consoled by the fact that one sincerely tried to make amends.

THE EASY WAY OUT

WHENEVER YOUNG people get into trouble, critics usually blame the parents, the schools, society, economics and culture, among other things. People always need someone or something to point the finger at as the reason why things went wrong.

There is so much of this going on that people don't really like to be honest about their mistakes anymore. Because we are made to feel so guilty, we just prefer not to admit anything or we blame every Tom, Dick and Harry for every conceivable ill.

We don't want to take personal responsibility for failure. It's easier and a lot more convenient to shift the blame for our problems onto others. However, this attitude of side-stepping true responsibility in order to protect ourselves from criticisms prevents us from growing the way we should. It acts as a cover for our mistakes and helps to perpetuate our stupid negative behavior. When youngsters are brought to DARE, they almost always put the blame for their woes and problems on their parents who don't understand, on society which is "hypocritical," and the "lack of care" on the part of people in general. They hardly ever blame themselves.

And because they absolve themselves from all guilt, they feel justified in living their messy lives. Until they learn to take full responsibility for their actions, they can never change because they feel the situation is not of their making.

The man who is fooling around with another woman and who blames his affair on his nagging wife will go on until he is forced to break off or until he assumes responsibility for his infidelity. I have met so many married people who claim that their infidelity was caused by the inadequacy of their mates.

These spouses are most difficult to talk to because they refuse to admit to any guilt; they claim the situation is not their own doing.

There are the poor who say they cannot move ahead in life because they are without sufficient funds. So they sit back and take things easy.

Then there are those who maintain they don't have enough talent to make out well. Consequently, they don't even try to do better.

Negative criticism and blame-tossing are good excuses to do nothing. They are a lazy man's perfect alibi. They are also a curse on growth and maturity.

UNDERSTANDING DOUBLE TALK

I HAVE OFTEN said that "people don't mean what they say, and say what they don't mean." I'm not trying to be smart with words when I write this. Most often, people mean something other than what they say. Without wanting to and perhaps unconsciously, we engage in a lot of "double talk."

The heavy drinker will tell you that he isn't an alcoholic because he doesn't drink in the morning every day. The person who says: "I'm a peaceable man, but…:" is usually anything but a peaceable man. The woman who says "I don't like gossip, but…:" should not be trusted with your confidence. The individual who says: "I like you but…" doesn't REALLY like you. He who says "I have nothing against rich people, but…" basically bears hostility against the wealthy. He who says he doesn't need any help with his troubles is the one who needs it most. And most often, the problem we think is causing us pain is usually not the problem at all.

A psychiatrist once said that: "People always misidentify what their problem is." This same psychiatrist was known to repeat that his customers "were always wrong." He went on to clarify his remarks. "If you for instance, tell me you have to do more research, I know right away that the problem is psychological. If you tell me, on the other hand, that the reason for your not writing is psychological, I can be perfectly certain that it is because you have to do more research. That's the first thing you learn in psychiatry, that the customer is always wrong. If a patient tells me his problem is in the present, I know it's in the past; if he tells me it's in the past, I know it's in the present. If he says he's sane, I know he's crazy; if he says he's crazy, I know he's sane." The psychiatrist went on to add that when he himself is "the customer," things are no different.

If you really want to understand people, listen to what they are not saying. A woman once came to me with a problem about her son's negative behavior. After telling her that I was willing to help, she said she wanted me to talk to her husband first. To make a long story short, it became quite clear that what she really wanted to talk about was her disintegrating relationship with her husband, who was having an affair with another woman.

Straight talk is as difficult as it is rare. You've got to be able to read the smoke signals on the top of the mountain. They're silent but perhaps more accurate than the thousand and one noisy spoken words.

WHY SECRETS ARE KEPT

The reason we often keep secrets is that we imagine that if we were honest and open, others would not like us. We think that revealing our secrets would cause some kind of unpleasant consequences.

I think that most personal secrets are kept locked deep inside our hearts because we fear the rejection of our peers if ever the truth became known. We believe that others might get disgusted with us and turn their backs on us.

What we do not realize is that keeping secrets always affects us somehow and causes some sort of friction in our relationship with a loved one.

If I do not want to tell you my secret because it isn't nice and I fear that you may hate me, then I am keeping something from you that is very important to me.

This creates doubt in you and causes you to wonder whether or not that secret, once known, would make a difference in our relationship. This, in turn, will surely make you wonder what it is that is serious enough to warrant all this secrecy. Could it be that if it were revealed, you would think of perhaps ending our friendship?

Then there is the fact that when I keep a secret from a loved one, I feel insecure with the knowledge that at any time I could be found out and exposed. I also realize that this stress and tension could easily make me less comfortable with that loved one, thus adding to the strain that can be found in my friendship. The other guy may not even know that I have a secret, but I do, and it bothers me. This is what makes me uneasy.

I believe that if people only understood how damaging the keeping of secrets can be, they would take the risk and open themselves up more often. If only we were not so scared. It is better to take the chance and face rejection rather than carry around the heavy burden that secrets bring with them.

If we were aware of the distance that secrets create, perhaps we would think long and hard about keeping them to ourselves. If there is deep love, there will be shallow secrecy. If there is little love, you can be sure that there will be lots of distrust and plenty of secrecy.

To keep things from an enemy is wise. To hide things from a friend is folly.

A MATTER OF CREDIBILITY

It's amazing how people can be so untrue to themselves and still pretend that they are truthful. Take the topic of recognition, for instance. Tell a man that he's doing whatever he's doing in order to attain recognition from his peers and he will deny it.

He will say that he's doing it for God, for country, for his family, for everything and everyone except himself. Ask the wealthy man why he's giving so much of his time and money to social work and he will say: "I just want to help." The missionary who leaves the comfort of his homeland for a strange new culture will tell you he's doing all this for God. The soldier who volunteers to go off to war will insist that he simply intends to serve his country. The senior executive who is working himself to death says that it's all for his family.

I'm sure all these people are doing these things for the reasons they give, but I also believe that the desire for recognition is just as prominent in their minds. Recognition by one's peers is a basic human need common to all men. Few, if any, humans can do without it.

I don't know why it is that hardly anyone wants to admit that this is a reality in their lives. Perhaps it's because we have been conditioned to believe that seeking recognition is selfish and immoral.

I don't agree. People need to be motivated in order to move. What's wrong with doing things in order to be recognized for one's accomplishments? Nothing. As long as this is not the *only* motive for doing. This basic need for recognition spurs most men and women into action when they might not move otherwise.

The great scientist, Hans Selye, is unashamed when he writes: "I can frankly say that, as far as I am concerned, the desire for approval and recognition has been one of the major driving forces throughout my life... I will freely admit that I am proud as a peacock of the recognition and approval that I may have earned. And why shouldn't I be? Whatever I have done... I can't help feeling happy about it; just as I am admittedly unhappy that so many of my projects did not come to fruition... I believe it is below the dignity of an objective scientific mind to fool either oneself or others by denying that the desire to earn goodwill and love plays a real role in motivation."

Those who say: "I don't care what people think" don't *really* mean it. Of course they care. So many individuals try to make us think that the opinions of others mean nothing to them. That's not so. And deep in their hearts, they know it, even if they refuse to admit it. Perhaps it is because they want us to believe that they're so independent that they need nothing from others - not even their love and goodwill.

We should, of course, do things because of deep inner convictions and not just because of "what they will say." On the other hand, if the opinion of others can cause us to move on to greater heights, then why not recognize the value of it in our lives- and use it for a greater good?

OUR CONSTANT COMPANION

It is amazing how fear plays such a great role in our lives. Although we may not have the courage and strength of character to admit it, fear is our constant companion. We are afraid of life and the surprises it may bring. We fear death and the unknown that lies beyond it. We are afraid to love because we fear the consequences of involvement. We are terrified of loneliness and the pain it causes. We worry (worry is a kind of fear) about getting sick and being helpless and dependent on others.

We fear losing our jobs, our social standing, our prestige and our power. We are worried about the present and anxious about the future. Fear is such an integral part of our lives that we often feel forced to deny its very existence. To admit the extent of its influence on us would be to cause a devastating blow to our self-esteem. And so, we simply deny that we are afraid.

The mature man, however, has enough strength of character to admit the presence and the influence of fear in his life. He understands that it is normal for all men to fear. He realizes that he is distorting reality and deceiving himself when he refuses to admit his moments of fear and anxiety. Because he is honest with his feelings, he is capable of dealing with them more effectively than the man who twists reality out of shape. Reality- whether pleasant or unpleasant- does not change because one wishes it so. One cannot make a reality disappear by simply denying that it exists.

It is important to note that all of us make use of unconscious processes that defend us against anxiety. Most often, we are unaware of these goings-on within us. They are called defense mechanisms. Every defense mechanism distorts reality in some way, and they all involve an element of self-deception. Denial of reality is one such defense mechanism.

I remember talking to a man whose children were being brought up by his mother. I asked him why he had turned over the responsibility of raising his kids to his mother. He answered me by saying that he thought she could do a better job. When I asked him what he would do if his mother died, he replied, "She will not die." I asked him if it were possible for his mother to die before his children were fully grown into adulthood. He said, "It's not possible for her to die because we live long in our family."

This kind of thinking may sound funny to you. You may even wonder how a man can fool himself so thoroughly. However, if you knew how great was the anxiety and conflict within this man, you would understand why denial was a perfect defense mechanism for him. By refusing to even think of the possibility that his mother might pass away before his children could stand on their own, he was alleviating the tremendous amount of stress and tension that had built up within him.

The chain smoker who is told time and time again that his cigarette habit is harmful to his health may also use denial as a defense for his continued smoking. "I don't believe it. I feel great. My uncle lived to be eighty-eight and he smoked two packs a day. It's just not true." Now that he has denied the realities of nicotine and contamination of the lungs, our chain smoker can go right on puffing without excessive anxiety. By lying to himself and engaging in self-deception, he is able to bring down the level of anxiety to manageable proportions. How can he go on smoking, believing that he is killing himself a little bit more with every puff he takes?

When the use of denial as a defense mechanism gets out of hand, then you can expect lots of trouble. A man cannot go on denying reality for very long. Sooner or later, it is going to catch up with him.

THE WORST THING IS WASTED PAIN

We come into the world alone and in pain; we live in much of our lives in loneliness and suffering; and we leave this earth alone and in agony.

Pain, hurt, frustration are all a condition of life. We can never avoid suffering completely. Sooner or later, it's bound to come crashing into our lives. To hope for a painless life is to desire the unreal. To be surprised when we're hurt is to be naive. All of us are destined to suffer on and off during the whole of our days on this planet. This is a reality we must accept and learn to live with. There is no escape, and the sooner we prepare for misfortune and suffering to visit us, the better we shall be able to cope with tragedy, loneliness and frustration.

The key to happy living lies in being able to deal effectively with pain. The emphasis is on the word "effectively." There will be suffering no matter what one does to avoid it. How one handles it is something else again. Those who have never learned how to deal effectively with pain are destined to waste so many opportunities to grow. In fact, our mental institutions are jammed with people who were unable to handle suffering and eventually cracked up.

The mature person uses the pain in his life to grow ever richer in maturity. A psychologist once wrote that pain and suffering are the start of all changes. And change is growth. A mature man is disappointed in love. His woman leaves him for another man. Instead of weeping and beating his head against the wall, he looks into himself, his relationship, and asks what caused his love to fall apart. He confronts his hurt and challenges it. He fights the temptation to retreat and to run. He looks right into his suffering, bravely picks himself up and continues on his way in spite of it all. Thus, he gets used to doing battle with pain. In time, he even becomes hardened to it. He soon is skillful at handling pain and stress. Consequently, he is not deterred when faced with the prospect of deep suffering as the price of success. He is willing and able to pay the price. That's why there is nothing impossible for him because he will always go on in spite of pain. That determination will insure his success.

The worst thing in the world is not pain but wasted pain… pain that is suffered without anything positive coming from it… pain that hurts terribly and leaves a man bowed and defeated.

SOME THOUGHTS ON DEATH

I HAVE A STRONG feeling that not all of you who begin reading this chapter will finish it. Whenever I bring up the subject of death, I always lose a number of readers. Somebody once referred to death as the "awful certainty." Death is the only sure thing in life. There is no escaping it. It will come as surely as the setting of the sun.

Yet there are people who never give death much thought. Perhaps it is because they are too scared to think about it. Or maybe they know that death is the real spoiler in life and they don't want to think about their plans getting all fouled up.

There are people who never break the "death barrier." They cannot or will not confront their feelings about death. The world's greatest thinkers have always insisted that wisdom and happiness are only possible after a person has come to terms with the inevitability of death. I believe this is obvious to anyone who does a little bit of serious thinking. People who refuse to think about death begin to live and behave as though they are immortal. Refusing to acknowledge the reality of death is like saying that I will live on forever. This kind of thinking can very possibly lead a person to live in a world of fantasy, far removed from reality.

I personally believe that it is good to think about death at least once in a while. It makes us more human. It reminds us that we are not the gods we sometimes make ourselves out to be. It has a tempering effect on us. The thought of death also urges us to make decisions that we had been putting off. It reminds us that time is short, and if we are to make the best of all the days that we have left, we must get on with the business of living.

The man who has not come to terms with death cannot truly be happy. There is always a dark cloud hanging over him that is somehow watering down the joys that he may experience. A man needs to understand what death means and why people should die. Death is viewed by some as an enemy and end to life, the grim reaper. It may seem as punishment, the ultimate alienation.

Others see it as a prelude to rebirth, the hidden friend, the beginning of a new life. Many primitive tribesmen believe this. Perhaps that is why they are able to face death seriously and with a calm and serenity that confuses modern man.

Perhaps the reason we see death as such a terrible thing is that we look upon it as observers. A friend is here one moment and gone the next. There is a tremendous vacuum in our lives caused by loneliness and depression. Death seems to be so closely linked to pain and suffering that it is no small wonder that we dread it. If a loved one dies, then death is seen as a great enemy who takes away a source of love, consolation, and affection. When an enemy dies we see death as a friend who rescues us from pain and embarrassment.

All thoughts about death pale before the reality of it. I suppose one can never really understand it unless one has experienced it. And those who experienced it obviously have not been able to tell us whether or not it was a pleasant happening. I suppose the best thing to do in order to confront our feelings about death is to imagine that death is about to happen.

Suppose that you have just discovered that you are affected with a fatal disease. You have one month left to live. How would you feel? What would you do? What would be your thoughts? How would you spend your final days? What would you want written on your tombstone? Would you leave this world with a smile on your face, or with a curse on your lips? Would you be happy, indifferent, or resentful about dying? Think about it, if you dare.

COPING WITH INSECURITY

All of us are very insecure creatures. From the moment we come into this big world of ours, up to the time we are called out of it, there are countless fears that we have to cope with.

As children, we are very fearful for our physical safety. Everything and everybody is huge and we are so tiny, so helpless and so dependent. We really cannot do anything on our own. We have to be fed, clothed and given directions, even into the minutest details of our lives.

When we move into the adolescence, there is a whole new set of fears to deal with. The love and care we sought to gain from the limited circle of our parents and relatives, we now look for in a wider group of people. We feel the need to be accepted by our classmates, our neighborhood pals and even the strangers we bump into during our everyday life. We fear rejection and this gives rise to all sorts of feelings of insecurity.

We also long to love and be loved in an intense fashion. The females among us worry about not finding that "man of their dreams." They very often push the "panic button" when they find themselves falling out of love. Some have gone even so far as to destroy themselves because the whole world has come crashing down on them and they suddenly feel so insecure, so alone, that they believe that they must put an end to it all.

As we grow into adulthood, new fears assault us. We need jobs, good ones, to assure our financial stability. We need status and prestige and the acceptance of our peers.

Insecurity for me is a way of life. I am always getting those feelings of insecurity. I guess you are like me. What makes the difference is how we cope with these feelings.

Some of us become as if paralyzed and we just cannot seem to move. Some of us, on the other hand, can continue to function well even if we experience terrible feeling of insecurity.

I personally feel insecure often. When we start a new rehabilitation center, I worry about lots of things, from the money to the program. Every day I have reason to feel insecure. And the feelings do come. I can't help it. I guess that's normal.

Expect to feel insecure often. It's all part of the game of life. So many of us make the mistake of thinking that we are alone in our insecurity. We are ashamed to admit what we feel. We think ourselves inferior because we often appear to be shaky on our emotional feet.

The sooner we understand that maturity does not mean the absence of insecure feelings but rather the ability to function well in spite of them, the sooner we realize that success is possible no matter how strong our insecurity - if we know how to deal with it.

Feel insecure? Welcome to the human race. Don't worry about it. Rather, worry about worrying too much. After worrying for a little while, go ahead and do what you believe is right. More often than not, you won't regret it.

THE CONSEQUENCES OF SELF-PITY

WOULD YOU BELIEVE that some people work hard at making themselves unhappy? Is it possible that someone who can see misery around the corner would still make the turn? The answer is a definite and resounding ***yes***.

Why in the world would any individual prefer to be unhappy when he could enjoy himself? Only because he believes that by being unhappy now, he can reap greater joy later.

Take, for example, the woman who insists on prolonging the argument with her -husband when she knows very well that there would be immediate peace if she broke off the fight and remained silent. What does she hope to gain by carrying on and on and making everybody miserable? Victory, ultimate victory.

Have you ever heard of a war of attrition? It means wearing down your enemy over a long period of time by continuous and unending conflict. It means being willing to take punishment and suffering in order to ultimately win out.

The woman who always nags her husband about his drinking realizes full well that every time he comes home drunk, there will be unpleasantness. However, she is willing to risk it anyway because she hopes that somehow her words will penetrate and have some effect on the man.

People who pity themselves do so for much the same reason. They make themselves unhappy hoping that somebody will come along and see their misery and do something about it. Do what? Give them much needed attention, of course.

However, this game is dangerous indeed. Aside from suffering during the expected time, there is also the very real chance that there is no Good Samaritan on the horizon.

What happens if there isn't? Nothing except a greater degree of misery, which results in a more intense feeling of frustration and depression.

What about the person who is constantly wallowing in self-pity? He soon finds himself with few real friends. Most mature people get sick and tired of playing his emotionally expensive game. Aside from the do-gooders who are out to practice charity, few care to get involved with such a crippled personality that is forever in need of emotional first aid.

In the end, the person who seeks to be pitied is indeed in a sad state. He remains alone, insecure, frustrated, and ill-equipped to do much about it.

BEHAVIOR UNDER STRESS

THEY SAY THAT appearances can be very deceiving. This is especially true when a man is tired both physically and emotionally. How many wives have been hurt unnecessarily because a tired husband came home after a hard day's work and behaved in a very clumsy way? I say "unnecessarily" because had the wife understood more fully the reason for his crankiness, she would not have been as hurt.

When a woman is fatigued or is having her monthly period, she is often a mystery to her husband, who is always trying to understand her unpredictable moods. Even children are not themselves when they are not feeling well. Try waking up a child in the middle of the night. See how he is impossible when he needs to sleep but cannot. It's not that he's bad, it's just that his body and sometimes his emotions are worn out and he can no longer control his negative behavior.

Aren't we all like that? Whenever tension and conflict move into our lives, we get jumpy and begin to snap at people. The tragedy is that we don't know why we are so angry. It is important for us to be more patient when the people we care for are tired and tense. We should be careful not to provoke them unduly.

People behave differently when under stress. Most of the time, some nastiness surfaces. A waiter drops soup on the suit of a calm, distinguished-looking gentleman. He explodes and behaves in a very troubled, undistinguished and ungentlemanly way. The sudden stress is too much to control, and the waiter is subjected to a terrible tongue-lashing for making an honest mistake. A man has had conflict with his boss in the office. He comes home and shouts at his wife because she is slow in bringing him a cup of coffee. The guy cannot handle the frustrations of his work and his bitterness, born of stress, spills out onto all those people around him, innocent and guilty alike.

When a child is cranky, we tell his mother to put him to bed. When an adult is constantly irritable for no apparent reason, we urge him to take a vacation because we know that he is not himself. We easily forgive people when we realize that they are not well. The kind and compassionate nurse who gets shouted at by tense doctors and scolded by sick patients is a classic example of one who understands and forgives.

What is tragic is that so many of us forget and don't realize these things. We react adversely and in an exaggerated fashion to people who don't really mean to hurt but who do so in spite of themselves.

Ironically, we often respond unreasonably to those people because we are not ourselves. And when two people who are not themselves are in conflict, you can expect big trouble. In the end, when the dust settles and both return to their right senses, there will be lots of fences in need of mending. That is the price of losing one's temper and not being able to deal properly with stress.

FEAR: A COMMON BEDFELLOW

WHENEVER I TALK to people about fear, I always get a sympathetic response. People somehow feel good when they hear a man speak openly about his fears. Perhaps it is because everybody is a lot more fearful than they care to admit. Or maybe it is because it feels good to know that one is not alone in his fears.

I remember when I was a kid, how I used to think that I was the only person on the face of this earth with so many fears. Everybody around me seemed to be so fearless that the thought that I was so different only served to add to my already existing fears. It was later on when I came to know something about what is in the heart of man that I understood how fear is a common bedfellow of men. I also came to realize that there are certain fears that are universal among all men. The greatest of these is the fear of death - the death of oneself, or of loved ones. Everybody at one time or another fears death. This is as sure as the rising sun.

Every single day of our lives, we experience fear. I doubt that anyone is an exception. I personally spend my life fighting off fear and striving to overcome it. What fears? All kinds of fears. Some rational, some imagined, some great, some small, some significant and some unbelievably petty.

But I'm not alone in my fears. I share them with the rest of humanity. The man who is afraid to lose his job; the teenager who fears rejection by his peer group; the wife who is terrified of losing her husband; the actress who worries about her popularity; the old man who wonders about his security in the sunset years of his life; the Pope who carries a burden of five hundred million Catholics on his shoulders; all of them have one thing in common-- they fear.

Men are all equal inasmuch as they experience the frightful feeling that fear brings about. What sets one man apart from the other is the way he copes with his fears, the manners in which he deals with them.

The man who spends his day worrying about death is afraid. He cannot sleep nights. He dies a thousand deaths before the real thing comes upon him. He is unhappy and miserable. Then there is the man who also fears death but approaches the inevitability of it all in a different way indeed.

William Shakespeare wrote in the tragedy of "Julius Caesar":

"Cowards die many times before their deaths;
The valiant never taste of death, but once.
Of all the wonders that I yet have heard,
It seems to me most strange that man should fear;
Seeing that death, a necessary end,

Will come when it will come."

A man can allow fear to dominate his life. He can allow it to poison his whole being. Unless he learns to attack his fears and crush them, he runs the terrible risk of having his whole thinking process contaminated and ruled by anxiety.

Perhaps the most important factor in overcoming fears is getting up enough courage to admit that they exist. You cannot fight someone you do not acknowledge as your enemy. Neither can you fight a shadow or a figment of your imagination. To admit that you are afraid is half the battle won. The greatest and bravest heroes will tell you honestly that when they performed their heroic deeds, they were deathly afraid. What made the difference was that they were able to overcome their fears. They resisted the urge to break away and run from the scene. They stood their ground and did battle. They fought the good fight and won.

Overcoming fear does not call for very much intelligence. What is necessary is guts. What is called for is the ability to march forward when one senses the strong urge to retreat.

When one can stand his ground and fight, it is amazing how the answers to so many questions suddenly make their appearance. It is unbelievable how swiftly and decisively fear can be defeated.

Perhaps it is because most of our fears are imagined and without foundation. The moment we challenge them, more often than not, we discover that they are not nearly as powerful as we thought them to be. It isn't very difficult to defeat an imagined enemy. When I cannot find him, in spite of all my efforts, I am immediately forced to admit that I cannot be hurt by a fantasy. The next time fear challenges you, call his bluff.

THE STANDSTILL GAME

THE OTHER DAY, I learned about a very deadly game. It is called the "standstill game." This game is played by people of all ages and coming from every walk of life.

People who play the standstill game are those who spend an enormous amount of time sitting nervously on a fence. They just cannot make up their minds. They cannot decide to move along the fence, cannot decide which side to go. They are afraid to move forward and don't want to go backwards. They would like to do something with their lives. They know they have a number of alternatives. However, they just cannot decide which one to take. So, they stand still. They simply freeze.

People who play the standstill game are very often extremely intelligent. What is lacking in them is not brains, but the ability to make decisions. No matter how often they think and rethink their situation, they just cannot seem to tell themselves to move ahead in one direction or another. They continuously mull over their problems and, when a solution comes to mind, they hesitate for fear that there might be a better one to come.

Indecision is the greatest problem of those who regularly play the standstill play. From their youth, they have had people around them who have always been conveniently situated to make their important decisions for them. They have never really learned to decide for themselves. And so, when left alone, they resort to the standstill game.

People who cannot seem to make up their minds suffer a great deal from their own indecision. They are aware of their lack of courage. They know very well that useless they learn to make up their minds, they will forever be sitting on the fence of life.

What we need to avoid is having grownups who become consistent losers and who are always playing the standstill game. We have to teach young people how to make decisions. When children are taught decision-making from their earliest years, they become adept at weighing all sides of the question before making up their minds. We all understand that decision-making involves a certain amount of risk. And it is these risks that scare people. People often cannot make up their minds for fear of doing the wrong thing.

And so, they play the standstill game and sit on the fence until they fall off.

It is always better to decide one way or the other rather than stand still. People who do not move get moved by circumstances that have a way of getting out of hand.

We are all capable of controlling, to a certain extent, our own destinies. This, however, means that we must make a lot of decisions. If we do not exercise this power, then our destinies lie in the hands of other people and in the forces that surround us.

We are all capable of controlling, to a certain extent, our destinies. This, however, means that we must make a lot of decisions. If we do not exercise this power, then our destinies lie in the hands of other people and in the forces that surround us.

No one makes the right decision all the time. We all take a wrong turn sooner or later. But what is necessary is that we take a turn and not stand there in the middle of the road sucking a thumb and wondering and being afraid to move forward. Countless battles have been lost by generals who could not make up their minds. The successful warrior is one who inevitably moves in a bold fashion. He is capable of making many difficult decisions in rapid succession.

So it is in life. Standstill game players usually lose. Success belongs to the men and women who know how to decide.

THE STANDSTILL GAME PLAYERS

ABOVE, I WROTE about people who play the "standstill game." If you recall, standstill game players are those who just cannot seem to make up their minds about a situation. They cannot decide to go forward and don't want to go backwards. So, they simply freeze and stay right where they are.

People who play the standstill game usually allow the situations to master them instead of being in the position to control the situation. Standstill game players are everywhere to be found, especially in marriage.

There are countless married people who are constantly playing the standstill game. They find themselves in terrible situations, and yet, because of their inability to make decisions, they resort to indulging full-time in the standstill game. As much as they would like to, they just cannot seem to find the courage to move, one way or the other.

Take Herman, for instance. He has been married for nine years, has three children and a petty wife. Herman has been very troubled lately because he is suspecting his wife is having an affair with another man. Although he cannot be one hundred percent sure, he has good reasons to doubt her fidelity. For weeks now, Herman has been wanting to confront his wife. However, he just cannot get the courage to do so.

It is because he might have to face the truth that perhaps his wife does not love him? Or is it that he just cannot face the possibility of the tremendous conflict that might emerge if he is wrong about his suspicions? And because of his inability to move into the heart of the matter with courage, Herman resorts to playing the standstill game. He remains full of doubts, suspicions, and insecurities. If only he had the courage and strength to open up his feelings to his wife, the whole matter might just be all cleared up in a matter of hours. However, because he doesn't have the courage required to deal with the situation, he becomes a tragic victim of the standstill game.

Or look at Linda. She is a charming and beautiful secretary who is very unhappy with her job. She doesn't like the atmosphere in her office and she wants to get out. She keeps telling herself that she can always find a job elsewhere. Her brain tells her that this is so, but she feels fear. She's scared to walk away from the protectiveness and security that she experiences in her present job for the unknown that she would undoubtedly face if she did leave. For months now, she had been toying with the idea of going out to find a better life. However, because of her insecurities and fears, she too becomes a victim of the standstill game.

It is absolutely amazing how many of us remain unhappy because of our inability to throw off our fears and make up our minds. We believe that no decision is better than the wrong decision. I personally disagree wholeheartedly. I think that the wrong decision is better than no decision. At least, one learns from a wrong move and can recover and move off in the right direction. So long as I stand around with my hands in my pockets, trying to make up my mind whether to move or not to move, I am wasting precious, valuable time. I'm also allowing learning opportunities to slip by.

One of the greatest emotional killers in life is the standstill game. It cripples more people than we will ever know. It causes them to float aimlessly through life. It makes them easy prey to all kinds of circumstances. It promotes indecision and causes people to die emotionally from inaction.

Beware of the standstill game. Few, if any players, emerge from it as winners.

CONFLICTS: A PART OF LIFE

PERHAPS THE MOST striking characteristic of the mature man is the constant change taking place in his life. Maturity implies evolution. It means a continuous process of emergence.

A mature man is forever becoming today something and somebody that he was not yesterday. There is something within him that calls for progressive change. A mature man is not satisfied with what he was. "Having been" is not enough for him since he is so concerned with becoming.

Perhaps this is why the friends of the mature man are kept in a constant state of confusion. He is changing and evolving so quickly that his personality is forever taking on new characteristics. What was true of him yesterday may no longer be valid today.

There are some people who, after an absence of years, return home and are pretty much the same. Their thinking has not evolved very much. They are predictable because their behavior patterns are, for the most part, set.

Things are not so in the case of the mature man. There is none of this rigidity. On the contrary, there is a flexibility and an openness which characterize his thinking and his behavior. Maturity means growth. And growth can move in many directions. This is why there is a need for that "spirit of exploration." The mature man is willing to strike out into the unknown. He has the courage to do things differently in order to gain new insights. He understands that in order to bring about exciting self-discoveries, he must often break with established thinking and modes of behavior.

Much of what he thought was meaningful last year, he now finds meaningless. Many of the ideas that he felt were interesting to him a month ago, he now discovers are of little value. This is because things are happening in his mind and in his heart.

Things are happening in his mind and his heart because he wants them to happen. The mature man looks for change. He desires change not for the sake of change, but because he fully realizes that he has not achieved the degree of maturity that he longs for. He is aware that he has a lot of growing up to do.

The mature man compares his life to an unfinished painting. He is the artist who is constantly working on his canvas. Never satisfied with the present state of things, he is forever looking for means to improve, to evolve and to emerge.

For some, living with a mature man is exciting. For others, it is unsettling. People who are scared to grow, who are threatened by new things and who are uncertain of their ability to cope with the future are bothered by the mature man. He seems to be sure of himself, so willing to risk, so quick to change that he causes them anxiety. However, those who have a certain degree of daring, who are eagerly looking forward to changing themselves - these people are thrilled by the presence of the mature man. They know that he represents a new opportunity for emotional growth. They see him as a definite asset in their lives.

THE ABCs OF GROWING UP

EVERY MAN WHO desires to grow emotionally, intellectually and spiritually must take time out for self-exploration. There can be no real growth unless a person is willing to look into himself truthfully and honestly.

This is no easy thing to do. We lie to ourselves (and to others too) all the time. We do this because it is convenient to do so. We're also dishonest with ourselves because our lies are used as effective barricades against the forces of truth.

To face ourselves with the truth can be a very frightening experience indeed. Should a man look at himself squarely and discover that he is not the person he projects himself to be in the eyes of others, then the whole world of this person can come crashing down on him.

I have a book with a very challenging title. It is called: Why I Am Afraid to Tell You Who I Am? The answer to that question is: I am afraid to tell you who I am because if I do tell you who I am and you don't like me, then where does that leave me? So perhaps it is better to lie to you, if I don't tell you who I am. Then, if you don't like me, I can always change the image that I project and maybe that will do.

I remember how often I rejected the prospect of honest self-exploration. And I also remember why I refused to face myself, to look into myself and see the reality that is me. I was scared. In fact, I was terrified at what I knew I would find. I had feelings of inferiority, feelings of inadequacy, and deep-seated insecurities.

I had a pretty good idea that all these things were there, but I suppose I could always keep this shadow of a doubt that perhaps it wasn't true. But had I looked into myself honestly and truthfully, then there would no longer be any doubt whatsoever. And so, for a long time, I refuse to see; for a long time I turned my head away and looked the other way. I knew I was fooling myself and yet I preferred self-deception to the truth.

I think we all go through this same experience often during our lives. However, there comes a time in every man's life when this form of self-deception becomes so unbearable, so difficult to carry, that he is forced to come face to face with himself. At some time or another, the mask, the thick heavy crust, becomes unbearably heavy to carry. Then a man has to pull and accept himself for what he really is.

It is amazing how easy it is after a man has made the first step in the direction of truth. Once he gets himself into the process of honest self-exploration, everything becomes a lot easier than expected, and he gets his reward, too. The pieces begin to fall into place. The reality of himself clear up. The shadow of what he thought he was evaporates, and the true person makes its appearance before his very own eyes.

Although reality is sometimes harsh and unforgiving, it is never as difficult to accept as we expected it to be. A man may not be the giant of his dreams, but neither is he the dwarf of his fears. The reality of himself lies somewhere in between. If there are a whole lot of weaknesses, there is also that heavy measure of greatness.

Perhaps the greatest tragedy in the life of a man who refuses to look at himself honestly is the fact he lives in a dream world that is far removed from reality. It is sad that he thinks so little of himself that he feels he needs to hide. If only he could see the greatness that lies within himself, he would not need to carry the burden of his other self. He could be free. He could be himself. However, the price he has to pay is honest self-exploration.

IT IS THE MATURE PERSON WHO CAN SURVIVE

I HAVE JUST finished reading a touching but tragic article in Reader's Digest. It is a true-life drama of a young couple and their four-month old child. All three got lost in the forest during a blinding snow storm.

Wandering through the woods without direction, the wife died of cold and exposure before a rescue was effected. The tragedy of it all is that it could have been avoided if the young family had only been better equipped and more knowledgeable about the forest and its dangers.

They made a lot of mistakes that could have been avoided if only they had been more careful. They were ill-clothed and not very well supplied when they went into the woods. They knew little about the terrain, and yet they wandered about without direction. In short, they did not know how to take care of themselves and that ignorance got them into deep trouble, which eventually led to the death of the young mother.

Meantime in the same forest, a hunter was also caught in the same storm. However, because he was wise in the ways of the outdoors, he survived and walked out alive and well.

While reading this account, I could not help but be reminded of how true to life this story is for all of us, only on another level.

Life is often referred to as a jungle where the strong and wise survive and the weak and ignorant perish. I believe this to be true. On an emotional level, we find many people unable to cope with the problems and pitfalls of life. They wander around without direction and without clear-cut goals to guide them. They enter adulthood ill-prepared and "ill-supplied" emotionally. They do not have the maturity (and the psychological strength that it implies) to find their way. In the end, they succumb to the countless pressures, stresses and frustrations of the world.

Then, there are the strong ones among us. They are those who have achieved a certain degree of maturity and have ordered their lives according to a realistic set of values. They have definite goals and the emotional and psychological power to attain them. They know where they are going and know how to get there. Eventually, they survived and lead relatively happy lives.

I have often said that the name of the game is maturity. The mature ones survive because they can handle themselves and difficult situations. The immature and irresponsible cannot. They perish. Which is why the pursuit of mature living is so vital.

IT PAYS TO BE FULLY AWARE

People often say what they don't mean and don't mean what they say. It is amazing how little people say with words. Oh yes, we talk a lot. Sometimes too much. But do we really say very much?

How much talk is really a useless or a feeble attempt to provide a smoke screen for our true feelings? How often do we try to fake out people and hide the way we really feel?

We can very often learn a whole lot more about a person by looking for other telltale signs that reveal to us his inner feelings. The way a man walks is very significant. The other day, a young man walked into my house. The moment I saw him, I felt that he was suffering from deep feelings of inferiority and insecurity. He moved slowly, almost gingerly, with his head bent forward. It was as if he were trying to be noticed as little as possible. I felt that he was almost making an excuse for being a part of mankind. It seemed very clear to me that he looked upon himself as one of the least of the brethren. My subsequent talk with him confirmed what his body language had already told me.

Yesterday, I was with an executive at a large textile mill. He was giving me a tour of their facilities. I was struck by the way this man walked. His body was as straight as a ramrod. There was a certain discipline, a hardness about the way he moved. I could see that here was a man who had strength of character, a high stress level, and a strong sense of discipline. I later learned that he was a retired military officer who had spent twenty years in the service of his country. He watched over thousands of employees who were engaged in operations that called for strict discipline, and he did his job well.

The next time you observe the movements of people, notice how they walk. You may learn more about them from the language of their body than from what they say.

A couple of days ago, I was in a group session. I was speaking to a young man when I noticed the facial expression of a lady sitting across the room. I turned to her and said: "You don't like me, do you? You resent what I have just said." At first, she denied it. Later on, though, she hesitantly admitted that she had indeed felt hostility and resentment because of the way she had interpreted my words. I knew that this was so because of the change that came over her face.

All of us are aware that these things happen. However, our awareness is not as great as it could be. If only we trained ourselves to watch more closely, our lives would become more interesting and filled with a deeper sense of satisfaction.

THE ROAD TO MATURITY

EVERYBODY TALKS about maturity. Perhaps it is because society places such a high value on being mature. Parents keep telling their children that they must behave in an adult manner. Adults remind one another that they must act their age. What people of all ages seem to be looking for is maturity.

Maturity, however, means different things to different people. The term itself seems to be very vague and misunderstood. There is a lot of confusion about the usage of the word. What might be looked upon as mature behavior by one is considered childish by another.

Some people believe that the moment a man attains the age of 21, he suddenly becomes a mature person. These people have a tendency to look at maturity in terms of physical growth and brute strength. Their concept of maturity is extremely vague and very confused. They look upon the "Marlboro Cowboy" as a mature man because he looks mature. Their concept of maturity is highly superficial.

At this point, I would like to take a closer look at the mature person. Although every human being is unique and different, there is a certain commonalty that is found in every mature person. Though no man can claim to be an expert in dissecting human beings, there are, I think, certain traits that are common to every mature person. I offer these comments to you for your consideration.

The mature man (woman) is forever moving towards a greater openness in his outlook. He is slowly, but surely, emerging from his cocoon of narrow thinking. There are new vistas, new horizons that are constantly opening up before him. New insights and self-discoveries become an integral part of his daily life. Far from being stagnant, he finds life exciting, vital and dynamic. He feels that he has a lot of living to do. He cannot be sure where his growth and maturity will lead him, but he is willing to take risks because he knows that he has no other choice if he is to live a full life.

The mature man tends to move away from facades. He dislikes "putting up a front."

Although he has been conditioned since he was a child to do what he has been taught people expect him to do, he slowly disengages himself from this kind of thinking. He struggles to rid himself of all pretense because he understands that he can never attain real maturity unless he has the freedom to be himself. Although he is tolerant of people who engage in superficiality, pretense and defensiveness because he understands that they have been conditioned to be such, he struggles valiantly to resist the temptations to do likewise.

Another common characteristic found in all mature men is the tendency they have to move away from meeting the expectations of others. We have all been brought up from earliest childhood to conform to the expectations of our families and of society. We have been programmed, so to speak, to do things in order to please others. It may often happen that we violate our conscience in order to please others. And how often have we been untrue to ourselves because we have said and done things we have really not believed in? Our lives are, for the most part, directed by what people expect of us. Even the smallest detail of our behavior is programmed by the family and society.

Mature men as a group tend to shy away from pleasing others for the sake of pleasing them. Being real and true to himself is positively valued by the mature man. He tends to move towards being himself, expressing his real feelings and being what he is. He allows himself to indulge in a creativeness that could run the risk of disapproval by the group. He refuses to suppress and repress his real self, although he is careful not to hurt or unduly trouble other people. He finds ways and means to ensure his growth and development.

This is not an easy task. It takes deep courage and a healthy dose of self-confidence. It means being in possession of a kind of spirit of adventure. Somewhat like the one that spurred the early explorers and great scientists on to their great discoveries.

GAINING MATURITY IS NOT EASY

I WOULD LIKE to present for your consideration a few more thoughts on the topic of maturity. A child is immature. We all know this. Because of his lack of maturity, his life is not really self-directed. On the contrary, just about everybody except himself makes the decisions about his life.

Mother tells him to do this. Father tells him to do that. His big brother orders him around. Everybody decides for him. The child is reduced to following the dictates of others.

When he grows into adolescence, the youngster seems to realize that unless he makes up his own mind about people and things, he will forever be a child. And so, he struggles to be free. This is most often interpreted as open rebellion against authority. It may be just that, but it could also be that the youngster is striving for maturity.

Every mature man values self-direction. He discovers an increasing pride and confidence in making his own choices. He is evermore deeply involved in guiding his own life, making his own destiny. The mature man can afford to do this because he is not about to be reduced to a slavish dependency on others. He has learned how to stand on his two feet. He need not rely as much on the wisdom of others as when he was a child. He has great self-confidence that his judgments will lead him on to a happy and successful life. He seeks the counsel of others. He hears their opinions and their good advice. However, he reserves for himself the right to decide matters that concern him and his future.

There is another thing that all mature men have in common. They value one's self, one's own feelings. If in the past he had poor self-image, this is no longer the case. He now sees himself as a human being with intrinsic worth. He realizes that he is a person of great worth in the eyes of God and his fellowmen. He does not indulge in self-pity, in self-depreciation. He does not spend a lot of time knocking himself down. He believes that, when God created him, He meant him to be a definite asset to his world.

A mature man enjoys the excitement of *becoming*. It isn't only achieving a goal that is of importance, but the excitement and the adventure of getting there that is very much valued. The mature man enjoys discovering his potentialities. He thrills in doing things that cause his hidden talents and potentials to emerge. That is why I say that he enjoys "becoming"

Perhaps more than anything else, the mature man places great value on openness to all his inner and outer experiences. He is very sensitive to his own inner reactions and feelings, the reactions and feelings of others, and the realities of the objective world. He is tolerant and broad-minded because he does not feel threatened by people and ideas that are different. He has enough self-assurance to carry him through possible criticisms and rejection,

The mature man comes to appreciate others for what they are, just as he has come to appreciate himself for what he is. He does not belittle his ideas that are foreign to him simply because he does not understand them. He is open and curious, and it is this very openness and curiosity that leads him from one discovery to another. It is this wide vision of people and things that allows him to grow with an ever- increasing rapidity.

Finally, the mature man places much value on relationships. He has great need to achieve a close, intimate, real, fully communicative relationship with another person. Shallow friendship is not enough for him. Superficiality in his dealings with others leaves him empty. He longs for deep and meaningful ties with other people and he is willing to go any length in order to get them.

The mature man is a very exciting person indeed. However, since maturity is not easy to come by, the mature man is, I believe, relatively rare. Perhaps this is the reason why he is sought after by so many.

THE HEALTHY PEOPLE AMONG US

IN A WAY, I feel guilty. Looking back on the many lines that I have written, I have come to realize that I have spent so much time writing about what's wrong with people, I have hardly mentioned what's right about them. In other words, I have tried to look at problem people and attempted to comment on the troubles that they are having in their lives. Perhaps this is not always the best way of doing things.

Maybe we should take a little bit of time and examine what we could call the "healthy people" among us? That is fine, you might say, but who is healthy? Isn't it true that each and every one of us is deficient in many ways? People say that "perfection is not of this world." Who can deny this?

Dr. Abraham Maslow, one of the world's foremost psychologists, decided to study the mentally healthy people for a change. Scientists are so fixed on the study of mental illness that not much has been written about those among us who are well. Maslow discovered that the mature, successful and happy people who had made full use of their talents, capabilities and potentialities seemed to be fulfilling themselves most. Maslow made an in-depth study of these people and came up with certain traits and characteristics common to all of them. I would like to base my comments on a few of the results of Maslow's studies.

For instance, Maslow discovered that probably the most universal and common aspect of these superior people is their ability to see life clearly. To see it as it really is and not the way they would like to be. They are more objective and less emotional in their observations. Not that they are insensitive, but their minds perceive clearly and tend to be less obscured by the fog that is generated by intense feelings. Most people have a very great difficulty to see things and people objectively. Often, distortions are created by their own attempts to arrive at objectively.

Mature people have an above average ability to judge others correctly and see through the camouflage, the phony and the fake. They are not easily deceived by sweet talk, fast operators and superficial persons. They are quick to detect the sincere individual and to set him apart from those who are "playing games." They are turned off by shallow people even though they may be persons of wealth and position. They prefer the company of the simple, the honest and the straight forward.

Because of their superior perception, mature and self-actualizing people have a clear notion of what is right and what is wrong. They have an amazing ability to "penetrate and see concealed and confused realities more swiftly and accurately than average individuals."

And yet they are not arrogant. They possess a humility and an ability to listen carefully to others and to try to learn as much as possible from them. They admit that knowledge and truth can come from even the most unexpected source. They are not impressed by degrees and diplomas, for they have found truth among the simple and the seemingly ignorant.

Consequently, mature and superior people are very tolerant of new and unfamiliar ideas. They are open and quick to listen to novel concepts that are totally foreign to them. They can do this because they are sufficiently self-confident to the point that they do not feel threatened to hear opposite points of view and because they have enough strength of character and conviction that allow them to accept or to reject them. Should new information cause them to change their way of thinking, they do not hesitate to do so because they possess the necessary strength to shift to another gear and strike out in a new direction. Persons of weaker character would more often close their minds to anything that would trouble them enough to cause them to think of changing their ways for fear that the necessary effort would be too much for them to handle.

Without exception, Maslow found that the superior people that he studied were dedicated to some kind of work, duty or vocation which they considered important. All of them enjoyed their work so much that the usual distinction between work and play became blurred. A full and healthy commitment to something meaningful was a common trait in all matured and successful people that Maslow observed. Discipline, hard work, training and postponement of pleasure were characteristics common to them all.

SUPERIOR MEN AND WOMEN

IN THE ABOVE chapter, I commented on some of the findings of the noted psychologist, Dr. Abraham Maslow, in his study of superior men and women. I would like to continue examining those traits and characteristics of mentally healthy people in the hope that we can all look up to them as our models and guides to future personal growth and development.

Maslow found that a universal characteristic of all the self-actualizing people that he studied was creativity. And the characteristics associated with this creativity were flexibility, spontaneity, courage, willingness to make mistakes, openness and humility.

These superior people were flexible enough to find new and fresh approaches to doing and thinking. They had that explorer and adventurer spirit that characterizes children who are discovering and searching for new frontiers.

Maslow found that self-actualizing people "are less inhibited and therefore more expressive, natural and simple." These people do not find it necessary to play games and mask their feelings and thoughts in artificial packages. It takes courage to be creative because the creative person has to stick his neck out and risk criticism and rejection from his peers. He stands a good chance to be laughed at the ridiculed as he strikes out in a new direction. It takes guts to be different and anyone who intends to be creative has to be different sooner or later.

These superior people that Maslow studied were humble and willing to admit ignorance and error. However, they also possessed this "stick-to-itness" that characterized every dedicated man who has a sense of mission. They were willing to forego popularity and consensus of opinion in order to pursue what they thought was right. In other words, they were so concentrated on the job to be done that they possessed the ability to forget themselves in order to get it done.

Great and mature people have the courage to make silly mistakes if need be. They do not excessively fear being laughed at. They fully understand that success is more often than not trial by error and rarely does victory come with the first attempt. Consequently, they are able to change quickly, to break old habits and face changes and situations without undue stress. In a way, you might say that they have a tremendous capacity to roll with the punches.

Although many of those superior men and women that Maslow studied possessed a natural genius, most of them did not fall into his category. However, all of them were hard workers who possessed a superior amount of discipline and training. They also showed high a degree of constructive stubbornness and patience whenever approaching a job to be done. Superior people, self-actualizing persons, usually possess a low degree of self-conflict. They are not at war with themselves. Their personalities are highly integrated. Because of this factor, they have more energy to spend for productive purposes. Since they are not focused so much on their own problems and conflicts, they are more capable of looking outward more than most people who are concentrated on their own problems.

This does not mean that the healthy person is unselfish. The fact is that he is very selfish in a healthy kind of way. "They get selfish pleasures," says Maslow, "from the pleasures of other people which is a way of saying that they are unselfish." I suppose you could say that the healthy person is selfish in a way which is beneficial to himself and to the society in which he lives. There is no doubt about it, we could surely use more of this kind of selfishness.

TRAITS OF MATURE PEOPLE

Maturing people are forever growing emotionally, intellectually, and spiritually. They are never the same after the passing of each day. They are in a constant state of evolution, always changing, ever growing.

Emotionally healthy people are creative people. In his studies of mature, self-actualizing people, Abraham Maslow found that creativity was a universal characteristic.

Maslow discovered that creativeness was almost synonymous with health, self-actualization, and full humanness. Characteristics associated with creativity were flexibility, spontaneity, courage, willingness to make mistakes, openness, and humility. In many respects, the creativity of these people is similar to that of children before they have learned to fear the ridicule of others, while they are still able to see things freshly and without prejudgment.

Maslow believes this to be a characteristic which is too frequently lost as people grow older. "Almost any child," says Maslow, "can compose a song or poem or a game on the spur of the moment, without planning or previous intent."

Spontaneity, also, is almost synonymous with creativity. Self-actualizing people are less inhibited and therefore more expressive, natural and simple. They do not usually feel it necessary to mask their feelings or thoughts or play artificial roles.

Creativity requires courage, the ability to stick one's neck out, to be able to ignore criticism and ridicule, and the ability to resist the influence of one's culture. Writes Maslow:

"Every one of our great creators has testified to the element of courage that is needed in the lonely moment of creation, affirming something new (contradictory to the old). This is the kind of daring, a going out in front all alone, a defiance, a challenge. The moment of flight is quite understandable, but must nevertheless be overcome if creation is to be possible."

Thus, while these individuals are humble in the sense that they are open to new ideas and quick to admit ignorance and error, they are also arrogant in the sense of that they are willing to forego popularity in order to stand up for a new idea. In part, this comes from their ability to concentrate on the job to be done and to forget themselves. They are self-confident and have self-respect; because of this, they are more concerned with the job to be done than with protecting their egos.

Because of their courage, their lack of fear, they are willing to risk making silly mistakes. The truly creative person is one who thinks "crazy". Such a person knows fully well that many of his great ideas will prove to be worthless. But this does not discourage him. The creative person is flexible; he is able to change as the situation changes, to break habits, to face indecision and changes in conditions without undue stress. He is not threatened by the unexpected, as rigid, inflexible people are.

Creative people are brave people, unafraid to go forward, undeterred by obstacles. They are, in short, the kind of mature people we all aspire to be.

WE NEED BALANCED MEN

MORE THAN EVER before in history, the world is in need of mature, well-integrated individuals. Society requires them because people are in need of correct directions that only healthy, well-adjusted individuals can give. We, who have to form the young generation today into a group of matured individuals who would be capable of tackling the immensely complex problems of tomorrow, must study the superior men and women who have come before us and who are still among us. Then, we can learn from them and we can follow the path which leads to maturity and a creative life.

A common denominator that was possessed by all superior people that Dr. Abraham Maslow studied was a life that could be called spiritual. Only one was an acknowledged atheist. Although many of the mature people in his study were not religious in the conventional sense of the word, they nevertheless led deeply spiritual lives. Nearly all had clear ideas of right and wrong. The characteristics of these highly developed people were similar in many respects to the values and ideas taught by the great religions. The saints are surely to be counted among the superior people.

The average individual is striving to fulfill his basic needs for safety, belongingness, love, respect and self-esteem. The mature, highly developed person has gone beyond that point. He is obsessed with self-actualization. There is a tremendous drive that has its source deep within himself that spurs him on to ever greater development of self. He looks beyond what most people feel are basic necessities. He explores avenues and frontiers that most people are not even aware exist.

The superior self-actualizing people, the type that Dr. Abraham Maslow studied, are a tiny percentage of the total population. In fact, they constitute a fraction of one percent. It is not surprising, then, that few people really and truly understand them. Yet, these unusually healthy individuals have a deep feeling of closeness to the human race. They can easily cultivate strong friendships regardless of race, creed, color, or political affiliation. They like many people but form only a few solid and meaningful friendships, usually with people of similar caliber and maturity. These healthy individuals are very tolerant of others' shortcomings, yet they are very intolerant when it comes to dishonesty, lying, cheating, cruelty, and hypocrisy. They can be bitter and outspoken adversaries where these things are concerned.

When looking for marriage partners, these healthy individuals tend to seek people with similar character traits, such as honesty, sincerity, kindness, and courage.

They also tend to disregard superficial characteristics, such as class, education, religion, race and appearance. Perhaps it is because these people are not threatened by differences. They can handle the pressures of non-conformity. They are more impressed by the inner qualities of a person than by outward appearances. They value meaningful companionship, compatibility, decency, considerateness, and strong emotional ties, and as they grow older, they place an ever-greater value on these things.

We must be quick to point out, however, that even healthy individuals are not without problems. However, their problems are fewer than most people because of their superior ability to deal with them. They are often temperamental and easily get bored with idle talk. They also suffer from anxiety, sadness, and self-doubt. They have a good sense of humor, but they do not laugh at the expense of others. They do not attempt to rise up by stepping on other people.

In fact, their relationships with others are never exploitative. Because a healthy person has a tremendous respect for himself, he can also respect others more fully. He who is fearful of himself is fearful of others: he who does not respect himself cannot respect others; he who is not sure of himself cannot feel secure in a deep and meaningful relationship. These healthy individuals are capable of cultivating unusually beautiful and meaningful friendships. Since they are not beset by the usual ordinary feelings of insecurity and inadequacy, they need to be cuddled and "babied" less than the average person.

On the other hand, they are more capable of giving solid and deeply rooted love than most.

When two people, two healthy individuals, fall in love, there is a far greater openness than in the average relationship. Neither is afraid to confront and be critical of the other when the need arises. This is because both have sufficient ego strength to withstand criticism. Both feel relaxed with each other and feel free to pursue their separate calling in life. Although they are different and unique, each in their own way, there is a distinct unity in their diversity. Both of them are one and at peace with themselves and the universe.

CHANGE IS PART OF LIFE

I remember what a nice couple they were. She was beautiful in her long white gown and everybody remarked how handsome he was. That was the day that they were married. They both knelt before the altar of God and exchange vows. They promised to love and to cherish each other until their dying days. They vowed to stick it out with each other for better and for worse, in sickness and in health, until the very end. That was five years ago. Today, they are separated. They tell me that they don't love each other anymore. I suppose they don't.

I remember a classmate of mine in the seminary. He was the brightest, the most disciplined and the most forceful of us all. He had always wanted to be a priest and went about it in a very determined way, indeed. He was regularly given responsibilities and positions of trust in the seminary. Everyone was sure that he would make it, and he did. One day, he knelt before God and dedicated his life to serving Him and His people. Today, he is no longer exercising his ministry. He is teaching in a school, and is married.

Remember the best friend you had years ago? Can you recall how much you cared so much for each other? How your love was expressed in a thousand different ways and how you believed that your friendship would last forever? Why did it break up?

What happened to these people? What went wrong? Why does love, friendship, and commitment have so many casualties? I mean, why is it that so many cannot keep love, friendship, and commitment alive for more than a short while?

Surely something went wrong along the way. There were changes that occurred and that seemed to alter the way of thinking of these people. And when people think differently, they behave differently. They take upon themselves new lifestyles. If the changes within them are superficial, their behavior will not differ very much from what it has always been. However, should they experience a deep, intense change in thinking and change of heart, then they will most likely be a radical change in behavior and lifestyle.

Because people live, they change. Promises of fidelity made years ago no longer mean the same thing. The commitments that were signed and sealed with sincerity a decade ago are seen in a new light. Friendship entered into long ago takes on new perspectives.

The married man sees more reasons than ever before to be faithful to his wife or doesn't see the point at all. If the priest does not feel a greater commitment now than on the day of his ordination, he necessarily has regrets.

Your ten-year-old friendship must be stronger today than it was on the day you entered into it. Otherwise, it has to be weaker.

As people grow, relationships change. Sometimes for the better, sometimes for the worse. We are not static. We are not unchanging. We are not like God, the same yesterday, today, and tomorrow. We are people... Weak, fragile, noble, brave, cowardly, insecure... We are many things, but most of all, we are changing. We are forever changing. Every hour of the day, every day of the week, every week of the month, every month of the year and every year of our lives brings about change within us.

The change may be significant or they may be deep. But there is no doubting that they alter our values. Values that were so dear to us that we thought would never change are now seen differently. They no longer appear to be as relevant as they once were. Priorities are reversed or reshuffled. Customs and traditions are abandoned because they have lost their significance in our lives. New values, priorities, customs appear to be more relevant than ever.

All this, of course, leads to a whole lot of confusion. These changes create violent emotional upheavals that shatter the composure of many people who are not prepared to change. They nurse all kinds of insecurities because of the many unknown factors involved. They also cause untold resistance because people fear change.

We are afraid of change because we cannot be sure of what it might bring. We can be relatively sure of the past, of routine, of the familiar. But change is unlike anything in the past. It is new and unfamiliar. Change means striking out in a new direction. It means risking and, to a certain extent, perhaps even gambling.

Christ was very much aware of this. Some people called Him are revolutionary. I prefer the term change agent. He caused people to change.

There are those who desperately try to stop change, inevitable change. They don't understand the nature of people. They have not studied their history lessons very well. They do not realize that they are attempting to do the impossible. In the end, they get stepped on and kicked around by the inevitable march of time.

You always hear talk about people and times changing. The truth of the matter is that most people initially resist change. They fight it consciously or unconsciously. If they accept it all, they do so only with great hesitancy.

What we must first recognize is that changes are going on within us all the time. We must watch for them and be aware of them as they occur. Some of these changes are of our own conscious doing. There are others that silently force their way into our inner being.

If there must be a change (and there must be) then, we would do well to remain in control of as much of it as possible. This is to ensure that we stay on the right track. Change can be a blessing. A definite growth factor. It can be also a curse to some because of its ability to cause devastation and ruin persons. Some people grow strong because of change. Some merely survive and others are destroyed. Change is inevitable and as necessary as the sunrise. We need it. What is required is the ability to cope with it.

GETTING TO KNOW THE REAL YOU

I NEVER CEASE to amaze at the fear people exhibit when they are threatened with the exposure of their true selves. It seems that they are deathly afraid to be known for what they are.

It is not that they fear showing the good that is within. In fact, if only they could spotlight the niceties, there would be no problem. It is just that the good and the bad are so closely interwoven into our make-up that it is well-nigh impossible to expose one without the other.

This is the great tragedy. There is so much good within us. More than we ever thought possible. Untapped reserves of decency and strength lie deep down inside us all. The problem is that we block the roads that could lead us there. We spend so much time and energy hiding the depths of our personalities that we suppress a lot of good along with the questionable.

In so doing, we have become experts in camouflage. We have devised and perfected shrewd techniques that enable us to hide our real selves from the prying eyes of those who would approach us to find out what we are all about.

Society as a whole has set up a complex but complete and very effective system of do's and don'ts that ensure that formality that has become for so many of us a comfortable security blanket. It is just what is needed to keep people at arm's length and make it that much harder for them to get in close enough to see what we really are all about.

Of course, I understand that these empty formalities are also necessary to keep at a distance those undesirables who would come into our lives without prior invitation. I am also a firm believer in that privacy that is every man's right.

However, what I am saying is that we very often use our wall-building techniques to prevent even our friends from getting too close. We use them on those very people who are dear to us.

In other words, we are hesitant to let even our friends know us too well. It is for the reason that we find security in hiding.

The real truth, however, is something else again. I believe that security resides not in hiding oneself, but in being more fully known.

The fact is that I know (everybody else knows too) that much of what you show me is fake. I know that this is not really you. I am fully aware that much of what you say and do has been dictated by custom and the formalities that go along with it. What I must know, if any meaningful relationship is to develop, is what lies beneath the surface. What are you like deep down inside? This I can never know unless you allow me into your heart and let me look around at things *just as they are*.

I realize this is risky and difficult to do. I also know that friendship and love are just as risky and as difficult.

Perhaps what is most iconic is the fact that if I could only get to know what you are really like, then I am sure I would love you, dirt and all. What makes you difficult (even hateful) is that three-inch mask you are wearing. It's not what you are that scares me, it's what you're not.

A MATTER OF IMAGE-BUILDING

"LIFE FOR ME IS LOOKING for the time and place to die."

This message was found on a wall. It was written by a young girl. She was 17 and a drug dependent. The girl scribbled a similar message on the same wall: "I now see life clearly, and it is something I cannot handle."

"All I see is more sorrow. It would be probably a lot better if I were forever stoned."

The tragedy of this youngster is that she has sunk so deeply into the depths of despair that the way out of her agony is extremely difficult. When an individual has such a low self-esteem, you can expect that kind of attitude.

We are, to a great extent, what we think we are. We have, over the years, learned to look at ourselves through the eyes of others. In other words, the way we see ourselves is influenced a great deal by what people think of us.

If I have been told all my life that I am a worthless individual, I will come to believe it. If everybody keeps repeating to me that I am an ugly duckling, then I will believe that too… even if it isn't so.

It is a fact that what people keep saying about us has a great deal to do with how we look at ourselves. I know a man who, in his youth, was constantly reminded of his faults. Trouble was that his parents forgot to say nice things about him. He grew up believing that he was really a "bad boy." His self-image was extremely poor. He had many strong doubts about his self-worth.

In the end, he became a violent gangster. His viciousness was matched only by his strong conviction that he was completely rejected by the mass of the people. He hated society and did not hesitate to wage war against it. He was sure that people did not like him. Consequently, he cared not about the hurt he caused them. He is now in jail. More than ever, he is convinced that he will never make it with people; that he will have to be in constant conflict with them. He will most probably die a bitter man with a giant chip on his shoulder.

So long as men are not loved; so long as people focus on what is negative and refuse to recognize the talent and positiveness that are truly present in others, men will continue to belittle themselves to the point where they become blindly unrealistic.

If we do not help others to see their self-worth, we will have countless men and women who believe that it was unkind of God to allow them to see the light of day; who feel that life is surely not worth living. Unless men are led to see their inherent value, there will be a never-ending litany of messages that testify to the despair and desperation that lie deep within the hearts of bitter men.

I am once again reminded of our young female drug dependent. Before disappearing into the city, she left a sad note that said:

"For years I had asked God to take me…
And once again I ask Him to take me…
And If I should die,
There would be nothing the world
Or society had lost."

GRATEFULNESS CALLS FOR MATURITY

REMEMBER THE story in the bible about those ten lepers Christ cured? Only one came back to say "Thank you." Of course, Christ was hurt. Just as we get hurt when we do things for people and they don't even say "Thanks."

How often have we been disappointed by people we helped! Often, they do not only fail to show some appreciation, they even demand more, and when they don't get it, they criticize and complain.

I've been thinking about this gratefulness thing. It seems to me that there is a need for a certain degree of maturity before a person can truly be grateful.

Children are not grateful. They don't appreciate a thing their parents do for them. They don't see why they should say thanks. They are too immature, too lacking in insights to see the necessity of a thank you.

When a man gains maturity, his brains tell him that what so-and-so has done for him is deserving of some sign of appreciation. And, because of this, the man expresses his appreciation in a way that is both proper and worthy.

Don't expect immature people to be grateful. They just don't have what it takes. They think the world owes them a living- pretty much the way a child feels. Or maybe they are just not humble enough to admit that somebody has helped them.

It's such a burden to care for ungrateful people. It's a "drag" as the kids say. About the only thing that keeps me helping such people in spite of their ungratefulness is a sense of duty. But, it's surely not fun.

On the other hand, what a pleasure it is to do things for appreciative people! They make you want to do more and more for them. It's not only lots of fun, it's even satisfying.

I suppose, however, it's those ungrateful ones who help us earn our way to heaven. Thank God we have them. Otherwise, doing things for people would be so much fun and so rewarding, it wouldn't be work anymore.

IT PAYS TO RELAX AND REFUEL

We live in a world of frenzied activity. From the moment we wake up until we prepare for bed, we go through a series of hurried happenings. The housewife spends her time rushing to and fro in the house doing all kinds of menial jobs. The businessman acquires painful ulcers before he is forty because of the terrific pace of living that has become his way of life.

We move so fast that we miss much of what life has to offer in our rush to get things done. We run past the bright red roses and wild flowers growing by the wayside. We spend a whole lot of time doing all kinds of things that in the end don't add up to very much.

I also have been a victim of this mad rush to get things done. It came to a point when my head was spinning and my heart was racing like an overworked motor. I got caught up in a web of activity that left me almost no time to breathe, much less think. I could feel myself riding in a merry-go-round that kept increasing in speed until it came to a point where I felt I would be thrown off.

That's when I decided to slow down, look around, and gaze into myself. It was really a wonderful experience. I spent a lot of time up in the hills of Antipolo. I re-discovered the beauty of the sunset and the exhilarating feeling that comes with seeing a fiery sky fall into the ocean. I felt the peace and the quiet of the rolling hills. I listened to countless birds singing in a chorus that was as spontaneous as it was inimitable. I observed little colonies of ants racing about, following the instinct that mother nature had given them. I marveled at the precision of their work.

I looked at the sprawling city below me. A cloud of pollution hung over it like a thick fog. I was happy to breathe the clean, fresh air that blew gently down from the hills.

It took some time for me to unwind. It was only then that I understood how essential it is for a man to slow down, breathe a little easier, and take time to look into himself.

I realize that a man cannot give and give without getting from somewhere; that a man can burn himself out unless he takes time to refuel and to recharge his battery.

I have always been a man in a hurry. Perhaps it is because I feel that I have only one life to live and I want to live it to the fullest. I used to think that to relax one day is to waste 24 precious hours. I have now begun to understand that a lot of wisdom can be acquired while watching a beautiful sunset or studying a bright red rose.

Bob Garon

While doing some reading up in the hills, I came across the beautiful prayer by Orin L. Crain that I would like to share with you. Perhaps if you are one of those people who, like me, can never seem to slow down, you would do well to clip it, put it under the glass of your desk and read it every morning.

"Slow me down Lord!
Ease the pounding of my heart
By the quieting of my mind.
Steady my hurried pace,
With a vision of eternal reach of time.
Give me, amidst the confusion of my day,
The calmness of the everlasting hills.
Break the tension of my nerves
With the soothing music of the singing streams
That live in my memory.
Help me to know the magical restoring power of sleep.
Teach me the art of taking minute vacations,
Of slowing down
To look at a flower;
To chat with an old friend or to make a new one;
To pat a stray dog; to watch a spider build a web;
To smile at a child; or to read from a good book.
Remind me each day
That the race is not always given to the swift;
That there is more to life than increasing its speed.
Let me look upwards to the towering oak
And know that it grew great and strong
Because it grew slowly and well."

NOW IS THE ONLY REALITY

In life there is past, present and future. It is amazing how little we live in the present. We spend most of our time feeling sorry for the past or thinking about what "might have been" or "should have been,"

We worry about the future and engage in expecting things and events that never seem to work out the way we had anticipated.

It is unbelievable how little time we live effectively in the "here and now." Of course, most of us are not really aware of this situation. We think we are living in the present. However, if you pause for a moment and honestly examine your everyday living, you will perhaps come to the conclusion that a tremendous amount of your time is spent re-examining the past and anticipating the future.

A Danish mystic once told the story of God sent the angel Gabriel to earth to offer eternal life in exchange for a moment of a man's time. But the angel had to return to God without delivering the gift. When he reached the earth, he discovered that everyone was living one foot in the past and the other in the future, and no one had a moment of time.

Perhaps if the angel Gabriel had offered me that gift, I also would not have qualified. I have been guilty of living too much in the past and worrying too much about the future. I am sure that in the process I have missed out on so many good things that the present has had to offer.

Oh, I am not saying that the past is useless. Obviously, the experiences of the past are the guide points to living in the presents. Santayana once wrote: "Those who forget the mistakes of the past, are condemned to repeating them."

What I mean is that we spend far too much time crying over spilled milk.

What is important is the here and now. Now is the only ***reality***. The past is gone forever. The future is yet to be. By the time you finish reading this sentence, two or three seconds will have slipped into the past. Those seconds now dead are given to the past. Everything that has happened has been swept away into the past, never to return.

For this reason, it is useless to waste precious moments of the present playing around with things of the past. Unless they have a direct bearing on the present, they should be given a little of our time.

The future is yet unformed. There is almost no way we can effectively anticipate future events. There are so many contingencies, so many unknown factors that can change the course of the future that it is almost absurd to give it too much thought.

To live today to the fullest is what gives a man his greatest happiness and deepest satisfaction. To consider the past without being focused on it; to look to the future without living in it; to give everything to the present without withholding anything; this is what *real* living is all about.

About the author

Bob Garon was born in New Hampshire USA. He was sent to the Philippines in 1965 to do missionary work. He left the priesthood and received his dispensation from his vows in 1978. By being involved in organizations that addressed the needs of troubled youth, Bob built a name for himself and is known as the Father of the Therapeutic Community in Asia.

As a writer and columnist, he has written over 14,000 articles over the past four decades. He has helped and inspired countless individuals and couples through his live phone-in counseling on radio and television, as well as with motivational speaking. speaking.

Bob also set-up a management consultancy firm, and, together with his wife Emmy, founded the Golden Values Schools.

Up to his last days, Bob worked with people struggling to overcome various addictions and helped them get their lives back together. He passed away in 2021 at the age of 85.

Thank you for reading!

If you received value from this book, please consider leaving a review, however short, on the Amazon page. This will help get the message to others who may need or appreciate it.

Royalties earned from this book will help poor children in the Philippines get an education.

* * *

OTHER BOOKS WRITTEN BY BOB GARON

Loving is Living
Love & Courtship
The Challenge of Marriage
Intimate Letters of Married Couples
Intimate Letters of Young Lovers
Reflections on Marriage

Made in the USA
Columbia, SC
26 November 2024